Billing
792-7000

Free Rose Light

9.4.21

Dear Gary,
I am glad this
book gives us
another
opportunity
to connect....

Our moments are
not great in
number.... But
always
an earth-
trembler
love Mags

SERIES ON OHIO HISTORY AND CULTURE

Series on Ohio History and Culture
    Kevin Kern, Editor

Heinz Poll, edited by Barbara Schubert, *A Time to Dance: The Life of Heinz Poll*

Mark D. Bowles, *Chains of Opportunity: The University of Akron and the Emergence of the Polymer Age, 1909–2007*

Russ Vernon, *West Point Market Cookbook*

Stan Purdum, *Pedaling to Lunch: Bike Rides and Bites in Northeastern Ohio*

Joyce Dyer, *Goosetown: Reconstructing an Akron Neighborhood*

Steve Love, *The Indomitable Don Plusquellic: How a Controversial Mayor Quarterbacked Akron's Comeback*

Robert J. Roman, *Ohio State Football: The Forgotten Dawn*

Timothy H. H. Thoresen, *River, Reaper, Rail: Agriculture and Identity in Ohio's Mad River Valley, 1795–1885*

Mark Auburn, *In the President's Home: Memories of the Akron Auburns*

Brian G. Redmond, Bret J. Ruby, and Jarrod Burks, eds., *Encountering Hopewell in the Twenty-first Century, Ohio and Beyond. Volume 1: Monuments and Ceremony*

Brian G. Redmond, Bret J. Ruby, and Jarrod Burks, eds., *Encountering Hopewell in the Twenty-first Century, Ohio and Beyond. Volume 2: Settlements, Foodways, and Interaction*

Jen Hirt, *Hear Me Ohio*

Ray Greene, *Coach of a Different Color: One Man's Story of Breaking Barriers in Football*

S. Victor Fleisher, *The Goodyear Tire & Rubber Company: A Photographic History, 1898–1951*

John Tully, *Labor in Akron, 1825–1945*

Deb Van Tassel Warner and Stuart Warner, eds., *Akron's Daily Miracle: Reporting the News in the Rubber City*

Mary O'Connor, *Free Rose Light: Stories around South Street*

For a complete listing of titles published in the series, go to
    www.uakron.edu/uapress.

Free Rose Light

Stories around South Street

Mary O'Connor

The University of Akron Press
Akron, Ohio

ISBN: 978-1-62922-127-4 (paper)
ISBN: 978-1-62922-128-1 (ePDF)
ISBN: 978-1-62922-129-8 (ePub)

A catalog record for this title is available from the Library of Congress.
∞The paper used in this publication meets the minimum requirements of ANSI/NISO z39.48–1992 (Permanence of Paper).

Cover art: *The Front Porch* by Nadia Alnashar, www.nadia-alnashar.com.
Cover design by Amy Freels.

Free Rose Light was designed and typeset in Garamond by Thea Ledendecker and printed on sixty-pound natural and bound by Bookmasters of Ashland, Ohio.

Produced in conjunction with the University of Akron Affordable Learning Initiative. More information is available at www.uakron.edu/affordablelearning/

Contents

Map Key

1. Front porch Cafe
2. Duane and Lisa's house
3. Main Event Bar (demolished)
4. Lincoln School Site (demolished)
5. Miller Avenue Church
6. The Pumphouse
7. Summit Lake Community Center
8. OPEN M Neighborhood Center

Map of Summit Lake neighborhood. Illustration by Mary O'Connor.

Introduction

When Duane Crabbs asked me to write the history of the ministry he co-founded with his wife, Lisa, it seemed a strange, though flattering, invitation to extend to a fifty-eight-year-old architect. Duane and I had only known each other for seven months. My focus at the time was helping South Street Ministries renovate the building they had accepted as a gift. It needed a lot of attention.

I have plenty of entries in the yet-to-do category, but writing a book was not among them. In one of those sad, sobering moments in my mid-thirties, I realized at the rate I was reading, there was no way on earth I would read all the books I thought I would read in my lifetime. That realization was so deflating, any idea of writing a book never occurred to me.

Before I came to Akron, Ohio, my architectural practice was focused on public assembly spaces. I transformed a lot of dusty neglect into performance venues, into theaters. While I was designing a theater on the east end of Long Island, I stumbled on a story in an attic. It would not let me alone, that story. Given the circumstances of its discovery, I thought it should be told as a play.

Within the small attic bedroom of a once-grand summer home lay the undisturbed artifacts and evidence of a search for identity on a global scale. Within the confines of a room undisturbed for over thirty years, the unfinished legacy of one life called out for completion. In addition to finding the family to whom the artifacts belonged, they approved my request to write the story of their mother, a story that straddled two world wars and several continents.

I started writing the play determined to stick to the facts of the discovered story. Eventually, it dawned on me that a play can never be a work of nonfiction. Writing a play is a creating a set of instructions for others. How did I miss that? The truth of the story is in the performance, not in the lines of text on a page. The writing is a map for collaboration at every step of the life of a play. My words were clues for the visual, structural, spiritual. It was just like architecture. I was painting a picture meant to be seen in three-dimensional space.

I improved the play over time and a few staged readings, but I still had my play rattling around in my collection of unfinished business when I moved to Akron from New York City. At the time, in my own personal life script, I cast myself as a kind of architectural hero. I came to Akron's South Street Ministries to renovate their building. Usually the client makes that decision, but I decided they needed me and—like some architectural savior on a bender—I uprooted myself from New York to Akron. Based on my recent experience as a Peace Corps volunteer, I was excited about pursuing an ideal that "everybody deserves good design."

Thinking the project might take two years, I saw it as a temporary move.

Shortly after I arrived in the fall of 2012, a group of us from South Street Ministries went to hear Anne Lamott speak to a standing room only crowd at the Akron Public Library. She spoke about the value of writing our stories, encouraging the audience to start it up and stay with it. It was a message delivered with humor, urgency, and inclusion. Ann Lamott made us feel like we could do what she did. I thought about my play. Before our group left the lobby of the library, I asked if anyone would be interested in starting up a writing group. Duane loved the idea. Gratefully, since I had only moved to Akron, he put together the group of five. We met every other week in the library of a church in West Akron. My goal was to finish the final draft of that play. By that point, I had been working on it for over ten years. During the five months the writing group met, I worked through the difficult sections of the play. I often asked my fellow writers to take on the characters, to read the dialogue aloud. The discoveries in the emotion evoked in hearing the words guided me to a deeper truth underneath the discovered attic story. By the time we finished our workshop, the play was complete on the page. It was so satisfying, that feeling of knowing the stack of pages honored both the original intention and all of what the ten years had to teach about how to tell the story. I could take my bow and walk off the stage.

Duane has a profound gift with words. He is a writer on his feet, spoken, passionate, and direct. But he discovered that the pencil-and-paper version of the ministry he and his wife Lisa created was not a story he could tell.

Then something unexpected happened. Duane asked me to tell the story of South Street.

For several years before our writing workshop, he and Lisa wanted to find a way to set down their experiences. There were some beginnings, but nothing had advanced. Though they barely knew me, the two of them trusted me with their story.

I told Duane I would think about it. It was a well-considered decision. I had enough sense to know that it would not be easy, that it would probably take more time than I imagined, and that I would need as much help as I could get. It was not something natural to me, a visual person trending to verbal brevity. Perhaps by birth order, as the youngest of five in a very talkative family, my tendency is to speak fast and skip to the end, lest someone snatch the floor before I can finish.

The acceptance of Duane's challenge came on a day when I was in a strange panic state. I was back in New York, my home of thirty-six years. I came for the memorial service of my dearest friend, a man I loved from the day we met in high school in his gymnasium at Chanel High School in Garfield Heights, Ohio.

I was on my way to Tom's memorial and felt terribly alone. The feeling kept growing—the kind of pushy, underlying desperation that drives addicts to use, alcoholics to seek the closest bar, anything to avoid what we cannot face. I did not use those escapes anymore, but I had the sweaty panic of need. I had to escape the murky threat, the impossible feelings.

My friend Tom had died in June, and I was now standing on a corner in the city of our youthful promise, and he was not there. Tom was the writer in our magical coterie of friends. He was the brilliant and handsome guy with a mess of problems he could never overcome. It was closing in on me, the agonized sadness of Tom Piechowski and its threat to awaken the deeper, scary spots inside. I was afraid I would not make it to the memorial.

My answer was to grab a distraction, quick, to get busy. To reach out for something to fill up every space and blot out the pain. It was my habit. I was good at it. And there it was, the invitation to write a book, right in front of me. Saying yes then and there seemed rational. I had been thinking about it, after all. It straightened me up out of the panic, erased the intolerable.

I called Duane and told him yes, I would write the book.

Then something unexpected happened. Duane asked me if he could say a prayer.

I said yes, held my phone close to my ear as I stood at the corner of Second Avenue and Thirty-Sixth Street. This was new. His prayer gave a kind of space and dignity to what had just happened. As my dear dead friend Tom was fond of saying, "It's the things you don't expect."

The journey of a book to its reading public is more like a tree than a flower. My own estimation of the time it would take was off by about six years. I thought two; it was more like eight. Those eight years are draped over the four years in the master's program for creative nonfiction at The University of Akron. Under the stewardship of my professor, David Giffels, and my colleagues around the table, I got better at recognizing the good lines from the paint splatters.

The writing was a life all to itself. A particular kind of solitude but studded throughout with the benefit of talking to people. Though my commitment to conveying the truth through facts was as strong as it had always been, as I got deeper in the work, I got deeper in the story. I was far from a neutral voice. Akron became home. I was writing about my community.

Throughout the years of my efforts, Duane and Lisa were open and available without a shred of literary evidence coming from my corner. I kept at it, interviewing, researching, writing myself into corners and out again. I wanted to get to the springs, to the source of their decision. I was following the line of how a courageous decision between two people can change the world.

One day in late January, I was interviewing Eric Nelson, the director of the Students with a Goal (SWAG) program. We sat in by the windows of a large comfortable lounge at the Summit Lake Community Center. It was late in the afternoon; the students were in the other room with home-work and snacks. The light was shifting dramatically, sunlight bouncing off the surface of Summit Lake and into the room at all kinds of angles, soft and warm. In the midst of that light, in a voice beyond the already-convict-ed quality Eric had, he said, "Duane and Lisa made a decision. But it was not the decision everyone talks about, moving into the neighborhood. It came long before that. It was the decision to choose obedience over comfort."

Well, there you go.

The storyteller is the one with the power, the one to move the pieces around, who makes the picture. The recognition of that responsibility in writing this book shook me, loosened me. I was able to show up for the third time Akron saved my life.

I was telling the story, so that meant I had the power and control.

The blessing of my freedom came through the explosion of the fantasy of such control.

What I came to find out as a would-be biographer was that I was setting the conditions for my true self to emerge.

Their trust was the essential grace of a breakthrough moment of the truth of my own story—the recognition that I lived a version of me that had been made up by somebody else. This breakthrough informed the story of South Street Ministries. I thought I was writing a biography, but in the soft-ness of the focused, often plodding work of building a book, I was writing the autobiography of a community. It included the entirety of place, of Duane and Lisa, the community of South Street, Summit Lake, Akron, and me.

Maybe this introduction is also the conclusion. Maybe everything I need to say about Duane and Lisa is that these two Evangelical Christians trusted a lapsed Catholic lesbian to tell their story. Maybe that statement is enough for you to know that you need read no further. Or maybe, I hope, you will take it as the invitation it is meant to be.

I

The Holy See

The Cuyahoga River sculpts a curving gracious break in the hills surrounding the city of Akron, Ohio. With green ridges crowning the edges, Akron is an airy citadel held in open hands.

What had been an easy way to get around town in New York City became something else when I moved to Akron. My bicycle became an instrument of ritual. It is the vehicle for reclamation of my history in Northeast Ohio. A bicycle goes to the speed of memory.

Pedaling around town expunged the ghosts and nostalgia of past places. Shadow and light are more easily separated at twelve miles an hour. At that speed, it's easy to pause, to take in any shiny moments along the path.

Right from the start of my life in Akron, the spin of bicycle wheels led me through an unintentional parade of ritual. It was all glorious to me.

One day, on a familiar commute, I was crossing from one side of the railroad lines and the Main Broadway freeway interchange to the other, a journey requiring the attention of all faculties. Scarred by its nefarious history, this knotty terrain once known as Hell's Half Acre still demanded watchfulness. The rail lines preceded the layout of most roads and buildings in South Akron. The expressway imposed a new circuitry over the old order. Simple physics of freeway design had created profound danger in the zone of the South Main Street I-77 interchange. The slashing, banked-for-speed off-ramps pierced the older street grid at odd angles, creating deathly unexpected intersections for the few pedestrians and cyclists attempting to cross the path of vehicles surfing in at sixty miles an hour.

On a lovely spring day, while stopping to ensure a safe margin of crossing time at this freeway nightmare I felt a curious sensation—a kind of space heater red warmth at my back. I turned and faced the dazzlement of a red brick building. She sparkled. The top of the building, rising above a tight curved exit ramp, proclaimed its name in giant, insistent letters etched in sandstone, "Akron Brewing Company."

I crossed to the relative safety of the island buffering the exit ramp. The crescent-shaped island is the largest in an engineered archipelago of banked landfills to alert freeway drivers of immediate entry to the city grid. I stood at the widest part of the crescent, populated otherwise by two dwarf apple trees in full bloom. In the direct rays of the setting sun, the horizontal light ricocheted off the red brick building and on to the delicate white blossoms. They shook slightly, as though the light itself threatened to shorten their fragile brevity on the strange island. In the oblivious rush of cars, my bicycle, the trees, and I shared the momentous bath of rose light. The petals glowed with free rose light.

An astonishment to witness, these encounters are the authentic God of noticing. Such moments shift everything slightly, so the world itself is not the same, it becomes less frightening. "Take off your shoes. This is holy ground."[1]

There are common hallmarks of action characteristic of every ritual. But the underlying reasons for enacting ritual sprawl in countless manifestations. Creating my own rituals served as counterweight to the rituals etched in me over which I had no control. I enjoy the formula of ritual while understanding that it is all performance, all artifice. The potential of ritual as a change agent comes through the artifice, through the familiar routine when something gets our attention. On the familiar, regular commute through a weaving crossroad in Akron, my attention was interrupted. I chose to notice and follow. From the familiar came the quiet extraordinary, the gift of the free rose light.

THE RIVER

The Cuyahoga River is eighty miles long, but the source and the mouth are only thirty miles apart.

How can this be? The riddle of the river's course is gentle and geographically meek.

The river is shaped like a child's drawing of a smile. From its headwaters, it flows south, but meeting the gradual rise of the Laurentian Watershed, diverts in a steady westward curve until the path of least resistance takes it north, to Lake Erie.

The Laurentian Watershed is a deceptively subtle land mass running east-west across Ohio. It is too gradual to perceive when looking at a contemporary map and undetectable if traveling by car along one of the roads traversing the crest.

Time spent with a topographic map of the area will bring the contour of the Laurentian Watershed forward. The strongest clue is the curious gentle turn of the Cuyahoga River.

There is the phenomenon of Summit Lake for another clue. The lake and the city of Akron lie atop the modest plain of the watershed. Water flowing out of Summit Lake at its northern end flows to the Cuyahoga, and on through the Great Lakes to the Gulf of the St. Lawrence and the North Atlantic Ocean. Water flowing out from its southern end joins the Tuscarawas, bound for the Ohio, then Mississippi rivers to the Gulf of Mexico. What that means is that Summit Lake is the wellspring of a long, serpentine, leisurely continental divide.

Summit Lake is an alluvial glacier-formed body in the middle of Akron. It gives no indication that it lies at an elevation of any stature. Across the long eastern flank, between the old houses and the Akron Municipal Housing Authority's Summit Lake Apartments, marshes still proliferate. Boggy stretches of impenetrable thicket blow the cool air of decay and buggy gloom onto the public footpath between the marsh and the lake.

The other deceptive aspect of Summit Lake's relative height is the long wooded ridge running the length of the western side of the lake in the Kenmore neighborhood. The crest of the ridge is part of the shortest path between the southern end of the navigable Cuyahoga River and the north-ernmost navigable Tuscarawas. The eight-mile portage was well-defined by indigenous travelers by the time it was incorporated into United States history as a treaty border between the advancing young republic and the people it needed to push west. Though it only lasted for fifteen years, the 1785 Treaty of Fort Macintosh made the ridge along Summit Lake the western border of the United States.

THE STONE

Sandstone is one of the most common types of sedimentary rock. It is still found in abundant consistency, thanks to the vanished sea that existed for millions of years, growing and shrinking and layering sand in a ribbon across the middle of the North American continent. Berea sandstone is the name for the local manifestation. It has a ubiquitous presence as rectangular dressed blocks in the older buildings of Akron, Ohio.

The voluptuous terrain throughout Akron made the consistent, fine-grained bedrock stone relatively easy to extract, and active quarries dotted the region in the formative years of Akron, including a quarry at the heart of the growing city on Main Street. The legacy of the tire industry and coal-burning domestic furnaces rendered the Berea sandstone buildings black. The recovery in postindustrial Akron has included restoring the stone. Though it naturally slowly darkens once exposed to air, the stone glows a buttery warmth after a cleaning. In sunlight, it bounces and absorbs light, reflecting the dark and light strains of its base composition, minute grains of sand.

In its natural state, it shows up all over. It shows up near the Front Porch Café, a freestanding building just off the corner of Grant and South Streets in Akron, Ohio.

Someone arriving for the first time might see little of interest at this intersection. Expressway traffic hums alongside. After the four access ramps were peeled away in 2016, McDonald's and Airgas Company closed, joining the other departed businesses along South Street. It was another chapter in accommodation for an old neighborhood accustomed to hardship. Without the in and out of the expressway access, the traffic light on the corner was removed, downgraded to the steady beat of a caution signal, then to a four-way stop sign.

Behind the Front Porch Café, the empty Airgas building holds one corner of the pale intersection. Across the street, the decommissioned drive-thru McDonald's has a brown fortress anonymity, a hunkered down island circled by service lanes. On the side of the building on the third corner, F. Cunningham & Sons carpet store has been shut down tight for a long time, though cars are always parked on the sidewalk in front. Above this single-story blond brick building, a giant billboard faces the expressway. On its giant flipside, for the benefit of the neighborhood, the message reads: WEBUYUGLYHOUSES. COM 800-44-BUYER.

The last of the four corners would seem to have the least to offer. The first impression shows nothing but a concrete base topped by a thick metal plate for something never installed. Behind a stretch of grass is the fenced-in backside of the Summit County Jail.

It's a place that reflects in miniature the subtlety of the Laurentian Divide. There is a low rise, a gentle, barely noticeable swell. There is a bald spot in the grass. There, the exposed Berea Sandstone bedrock curves down at the cap of the rise. The surface is dark, deeply raked with scratches, a glacial finish. It marks the southern terminus of the last glacier, the Hiram Ice Sheet. I was drawn to touch the manifestation of contained antiquity. Is it the proximity of the expressway that accounts for the energy, that warmth, the tiny hint of vibration? Or is it just the desire for connection to something that has endured, that will outlast us, despite our constant efforts to have it be otherwise?

In our desire to connect to the eternal, the stone conveys the meaning. We don't need proof. We don't need the Virgin's foot on the stone to understand grace.

"WEDON'TNEEDANYDAMNMIRACLES"

...just eyes to see the everyday.

The Speed of Memory

Akron saved my life three times.
The first two happened before I ever crossed the intersection of Main
and Market.

My invitation to come to Akron had nothing to do with its formidable past in my personal life, nothing to do with the first two rescues. I came to Akron for the first time on a sunny Saturday in June 2011 to see a close friend, someone I met in the Republic of North Macedonia.

Anne Schillig was one of the youngest Peace Corps volunteers in our group, and I was one of the oldest. Over the course of the twenty-seven months in the Vermont-sized Slavic country, we laughed our way beyond comrades to a deep friendship. We returned to the US on the same weekend, me with one suitcase, Anne with a hilarity of luggage and a loud Macedonian cat named Daphne. She returned to Akron, I to New York City. We were ready to come home, and home was a country that had just elected Barack Obama.

The Peace Corps staff warns volunteers that no one at home will be interested in our stories after about five minutes. It's true. So, for at least a few years, sharing barstools and memories with former colleagues is common and necessary. While visiting my sister Kate in Cleveland, I rented a car to see

14

Anne in Akron. It had been six months since we parted ways at the airport in Skopje, and I was looking forward to time together in her home setting.

Akron smacked me right away. Before my exit off the freeway, I crossed a verdant valley, crested a hill, and caught a fleeting glimpse of a large lake. It was this seductive series of views that made me realize that I had never actually been to Akron. How was it possible that I never came here, despite growing up on the east side of Cleveland, thirty miles away?

How was it possible? Aside from my immediate family, the two greatest influences on my life were both stamped "Made in Akron," and I never had the curiosity to see the place? Somehow it had never occurred to me to go. I didn't think of it as a place; I only felt it as a power. Now I was here, in an Akron that had a life of its own outside of my Akron, a place of two things only—Sam and sobriety.

Arriving that first time was the inversion of expectation. I was only going to see my friend Anne, and though I was in a car hurling through physical space at sixty-five miles an hour, the experience of arrival was somehow slowed down, a flutter in normal perception, a sensation I recognized, something to pay attention to, something entirely mystical. That moment was the grounding in concrete reality of something that had been, up to that moment, a completely ethereal connection to Akron, Ohio.

Anne lived a big old typical Akron rental house on Howard Street, just past the landmark she told me to look for, the Harley Davidson dealership. A huge contingent of gleaming bikes made it impossible to miss. The street looked a little sketchy to me. The dealership didn't really help that image, but I remember from a friend who lived close to the New York Hell's Angels headquarters on East Second Street that he said it was the safest place on the Lower East Side. Since getting off the expressway in Akron, I had already noticed a lot of bikers on the city streets. Motorcycles seemed to outnumber cars.

Anne was living in that post-college-but-still-like-college style with two friends, single women ready not to be single anymore. She had cultivated a fantastic garden in the side yard. She came from a farming family. It was normal to her. I love vegetables, but I lived in New York. I bought them. Walking across city grass with a basket to gather up spinach was astonishing to me. This was Akron: Howard Street, Harleys, and rows of crops in a side yard. That day together was reminiscent of life in the Peace Corps. We spent most of our time in Macedonia hanging around, just being with Macedonians. For a people short on money, visiting is the currency; warm food, homemade wine and ubiquitous Turkish coffee was their gift, their treasure.

Sitting outside, we ate a great lunch of spinach pie from scratch—made with her homemade cheese, the backyard spinach, garlic, and tomatoes.

At one point, I asked, "The Harley shop is hopping. I was blinded by all the chrome. Is that normal?"

"Oh! This is Founders' Weekend. Sober bikers come from everywhere. It's a big deal in Akron. There is a huge bike parade on Sunday morning to Dr. Bob's grave, happens every year for the anniversary of Alcoholics Anonymous."

Again, that feeling I had in the car enveloped me, one of slowing and grounding to place. I arrived in Akron during the celebration of the program that saved my life. I took this in while resisting what it could mean. I just noticed and stayed in our day together.

When I came to Akron the second time the following summer for Anne's wedding, I noticed more that could not be explained. During my third visit, I knew I was moving to Akron.

~

I was eleven the first time Akron saved my life. Going to spend two weeks at a Catholic summer camp was not my idea, merely another situation of bafflement that I accepted without question. I would discover plenty of reasons for me to love camp. Fundamentally, it was time away from Cleveland, it was outdoors, and if we weren't singing, we were swimming.

Before the first day was over, I also discovered a reason to pretend camp meant nothing to me. I fell in love. Just like that, on first sight, the full case. It's embarrassing only in that it is such a cliché; lots of preadolescent girls fall in love with their camp counselor. I encountered Sheila Mary "Sam" Murphy as the most compelling person I had ever seen. I felt something. It was beyond a crush; it was the love that dare not speak its name. I could not help it. I was just swept away. Unaccustomed to feeling anything, all I knew is that the feeling had to be mine alone. As long as I told no one, as long as no one knew, it could not be taken away from me.

At seventeen, Sam was a wild child. It was hard to imagine that this androgynous imp might have a home other than in a tree. She had a compact lithe body that defied gravity, like a spider. There seemed to be nothing normal about her whatsoever, a whirl of chaotic energy playing her coronet, a piper of charm. She carried an innocent defiance of the adult world while venerating nature and the divine spirit behind it. She inspired a kind of greatness and awe to those under her influence.

Just to see her in the world was enough for me. It gave me hope. Hope that even if a year passed, I would see her again. I would figure out how she would see me. I was determined that she would notice me.

I did not know anything about her outside of the confines of camp except that she was from Akron, as most of the rest of camp seemed to be. This Akron was fused to the feeling, to the love. The year I saw her, Sam had just graduated in the St. Vincent High School class of 1966. It was a time of tremendous upheaval in the Catholic Church. Born in the first wave of the post-World War II baby boom, Sam's personality and talents were emblematic of the surge of new energy in and outside of the rituals of Catholicism. Playing the coronet in marching band, she also played the guitar in the new folk Mass worship at St. Vincent's Church on Sunday and the Newman Center on The University of Akron campus.

Her intelligence and verbal agility were continuously undercut by an equal prankster instance on farting, burping, and otherwise causing discomfort or laughter in the midst of a serious moment. She could never resist sticking a pin in pretension of any kind. In the fall after the summer I saw her, she entered the Akron Dominicans as a postulant. Before the year was over, it would be clear that things were not working out for Sam's future as an avowed member of a religious order.

The contradiction of Sam was her status as an outsider and by her faith, an uncorrupted channel to God, a kind of direct current by campfire. The only time she seemed to be still was while teaching a song as she played it on a guitar. At such moments, her deep brown eyes would manage to connect with each person in the circle.

The sixties and Catholicism gave an outlier like Sam hope. Unlike the other burgeoning revolutionary movements roiling the country, the tremendous changes in the Catholic Church came from the very top. With

Vatican II, it was not the populous rattling the status quo and taking to the streets. It was the Pope.

It was a season to believe that real change was coming out of Rome.

In the United States, it was marked by the instant astonishment represented in the simplicity of a 180-degree turn of a man in a robe. On the first Sunday of Advent in 1964, Catholics in Akron and throughout the United States came to Mass to see the priest facing them and speaking English. That 180-degree pivot represents a turning point that changed everything in the relationship of the people to the church. Before that turn, the connection and understanding of the church they were born into had not changed for four hundred years. Most people accepted that it was always that way.

And the notion of change, of the potential of the faithful having some say was easy to believe in a place as free as camp. Daily morning Mass was on the schedule. During the high-spirited explosion of singing during the Mass, one or two campers might faint and fall to the concrete floor of the rec hall. The spirit was definitely moving in the room, but the fainting was borne of a more ordinary hunger. Mass came before breakfast. At camp in that era of promise, Mass willingly came before everything.

I was leaving that first year at camp unknown to Sam, but I somehow felt seen, or believed that I could be seen, that there was someone in the world who had made something available to me. Though I could not name it, share it, or wear it, I was forever changed by the vague encounter with Sam. It was the purity of it. And though it had to be secret, it was still an antidote to the equally inexpressible mysterious secret shame that etched a circle around my family.

I left camp with a new hope in the future. The hope that next year I would see her again. And I had fifty weeks to figure out how she would notice me.

~

Fifty weeks of private anticipation about camp managed to crawl past, and on the way to camp in a packed station wagon, my friend's mother was lost, trying to work south towards a crossroads dot on the road map called Bath, Ohio. I could have told her exactly how to get there. I traced it countless times with my finger on the complimentary Sohio roadmap in our glove compartment. The route was all surface roads then, and it took forever to get to the dot on the map. That dot represented my obsession. It was the last turn, right before camp, a mile and a half of Ira Road. It's a straight, gentle downhill course. The left-hand side was marked by manicured grass and the continuous white rail fencing of the Firestone family's fox hunt grounds. On the right, fields and farm buildings until Ira Road ends at the rust red painted gate of Camp Christopher. The stop sign is the final pause before the curtain parts and body and soul enter the eternal.

The mind cannot enter, but struggles anyway to get it, to name it. And we are a people of mind. So the question rolls on, what is this thing, so strong? If we were Druids instead of Roman Catholics, we wouldn't care about words, about naming it. Instead, we have made trees our servants and take up countless of their number to lay claim to creation, to find means of measuring the immeasurable, in words on paper.

In the course of the year before the station wagon passed through the gate, I had figured out how to get Sam to notice me. I discovered that I could be funny. I had a knack for comedy. While my girlfriends were recreating themselves to attract boys, I was making them all laugh. I found a way to stand out, to stand apart.

Passing through that gate at last, it was for me going from the wings onto the stage. It was a debut of sorts, an opening night for an audience of one. It was a place of suspension of disbelief, camp. No one knew or cared about the rest of your life while you were on those grounds, inside a notch of hills in a fertile Ohio valley.

The calculation was assisted by fortune. Sam was my counselor that year. The rest of camp was background to the main goal, to my not-so-innocent effort to capture Sam. Within the first twenty-four hours, on a hike, I scored a success. I made her laugh. Not only that, out of earshot I saw her reenact the moment to someone else. The plan had worked. The confidence of that moment was the charm to fully step into the space of someone I could seem to be. I made the deception seem natural.

The earth sparked as I ran through those days at camp. I was visible while invisible. The world seemed to curve away from this place of power, this confluence of soul energy disguised as modest red cabins and pathways through nature. The hot asphalt driveway to the mess hall exuded a sugar sweet air of spilled Kool Aid before it mingled with the cleaning compound, bonding in a distinct l'aire du campe. Every once in a while in the years since, smelling that particular mix brings it all back in full color, and I am there, singing with abandon in a pocket of time eternal, next to Sam.

Camp was the perfect setting for such aspirational fervor. Amidst the constant swimming and singing and strumming of guitars, there was an innocent current of sexuality throughout the reverberant echo of the enclosing hill. The perpetual swim damp subtlety of female ardor had me in a constant swoon.

It was confusing, it was brilliant, and it was private. I believed if anyone knew of its tiny light, they would blow it out. I never let on how much it meant, for fear it would disappear, be taken away without a word.

That was what I knew about love. It was dangerous.

My secret obsession with Sam, my constant nonchalant awareness of where she was in the world was really not much different than my friends' open worship of various Beatles, Monkees, or Kurt Russell. It was a one-sided fantasy. But unlike their unrequited love, Sam wrote back to me.

The year I got a job at camp as a lifeguard and swim instructor was the first year Sam was gone. After what seemed forever to most people, Sam was no longer a part of camp. There was autumnal reality to that summer. It was time for me to let go as well, my heart half gone already.

I was still in love with her, as I had been from that first moment. In the particular confusion of my endless journey to adulthood, knowing she was in the world was vital to me. We had enough glue through letters to withstand the departure of the place that connected us initially. Our distant link would have dissolved as well, but for my insistence as a correspondent. We were never personal in any emotional sense, but in our letters, there was a kind of erudition that must have kept it interesting enough to sustain the meager base and fifteen years of physical separation.

I wrote to her when I was in a crisis. Like the love I had for her, I endured my bewildering emotional territory alone. I was unaware and unable to ask for help. All I knew was to keep collecting good external indications of success, the good grades, the ambitious choices, working harder to compensate for drinking too much.

I did not know what was wrong. It would take me decades to understand, but in the meantime, I had Sam. Those letters to Sam kept me going when everything hung on a very slender thread. Somehow writing funny letters to her about a false version of my life worked to release me from the black depth of despair. Putting the letter in the mail, more so than receiving her equally chipper response, saved my life on more than one occasion.

For years, that was the lifeline for my tottering emotional balance. I used that rope until a particular morning on my rooftop in New York City at thirty years old. It was an unusually sunny day in November and while writing another upbeat letter to Sam in the midst of personal chaos, I recognized an emotion in me. I was...afraid.

Fear, like a billion other emotions, was not ever in my playlist. But there it was, right there on the tar beach rooftop with me. Instead of ignoring it, I told Sam everything that was really going on, everything. There was no turning back. I told her I had been in love with her from the first minute I saw her and still was. For twenty-six years. In fact, as pathetic as it sounded, I told her part of the reason I moved to New York was figuring that everyone at some point comes to New York, and I would see her again.

I mailed the letter, not sure if she would ever write back, but something was released in that honesty. I could survive on my own. She had gotten me that far, had saved my life when I had no resources to draw on other than her memory. I could let her go and keep living.

But she did write back.

Much to my astonishment, within five years of the rooftop letter, we were actually friends. We both had met someone. She and her partner Barb came to New York several times, staying with my girlfriend Cherry and me, in our tiny office/guest room directly below our tiny studio apartment.

Sam was never one to take care of herself when young, almost as though she was at war with her body. She smoked and drank with abandon tempered only by her partner's attempts to curb the behavior.

But it was not a chimera that I had loved. She was deeply committed to helping people. Sam, now Dr. Murphy, was a psychologist distinguished by compassion and a capacity to listen deeply. Her defiantly outsider status was a magnet to the marginalized. She was a counselor at Indian River Correctional, a facility for juvenile male felons. Though she lived her faith along the outside edge of the Catholic Church, she was a priest.

The two of us had a kind of tough guy way, an "aw, g'wan, who needs ya" relationship. We knew it wasn't how we felt, but it was just too much to express. On their visits with us in New York, simply being four gay women free in the world seemed miraculous enough, given where we sprang from. It was enough to fill our time with joy.

But I worried about her. There was a kind of toxicity to her body, a shroud of poison that bit by bit took her from a world that longed for the spirit she had been. I found it hard to understand how someone so good with other people's problems could be so neglectful of her own condition.

~

When I was invited by friends to Camp Christopher for an overnight visit during the last week of summer, I said yes. I had been hoping for such an opportunity. I could return to a place of such unutterable longing, but with a different purpose, a new context.

For a place as potent in my memory as Camp Christopher, hopping in a car for the twenty-two-minute drive was out of the question. My reasons have less to do with the fact that I have never owned a car than the need for slow passage through the buffer of time and space. With my accepting response to the beckoning, I began to cloak the experience in ritual.

There is the need for a script. When the ritual is a road trip, a journey, or a pilgrimage, next comes the map to chart the path. The trip to Camp Christopher this time was remarkably clean. Essentially it involved one left turn. I was awed by the simplicity. My street ends directly at the bike trail to Bath, Ohio.

The bike trail's official name is the Ohio & Erie Canal Towpath Trail, a triumph of imagination, persistence, collaboration, and brilliant simple design. The brief thirty years of commercial freight by canal boat in Akron was over by the Civil War, and the canal system degenerated from a connector to a local transport system until it was completely abandoned after the flood of 1913. Today, at all points along its renovated eighty-five-mile course, from the northern terminus in Cleveland to the southern point in New Philadelphia, people stroll and cycle on what had been the path of mules pulling the sluggish barges. The water is present in various forms; the confined remnants of the canal, the free flow of the two rivers that fed the canal, in swamps, and in the burst of the wide-open space over Summit Lake. It is an expressway of joy for walkers and cyclists. It is an artery of pilgrimage.

The simplicity of the one left turn. I get on the towpath going north towards Cleveland, get off the Towpath with a left turn onto Ira Road and follow Ira to its end, just in front of the entrance to Camp Christopher. It was a glorious prospect, sixteen miles with one turn.

Drawn by the enigma of travelling there under my own power by myself on a route more tree than car, more flow than stoplight, was more than enough to overcome the apprehension of visiting a place that once had such power in my life. It was a reclamation of some sort. It was inevitable that I would go there, but it was the invitation that gave it a purpose other than nostalgia.

It is necessary to pack a bag for this ritual. In my case, the preparation was simple. The necessaries were few: bathing suit, toothbrush, phone, money, and house key.

Setting forth, I gave myself plenty of time on the journey to pause as I wished. Ira Road winds across and through the Cuyahoga Valley like a stream, its curves and angles defined by geography and indigenous people creating paths of least resistance. Geometry also claims Ira Road, sharply defining the fields of white settlers with paper deeds of private ownership.

It is possible that those passing through in cars might be oblivious to its charms, but at the very least, the character of the road requires a slower speed and a brake-ready foot. Staunched throughout its length with out-croppings of human and geologic history, if nature does not get the atten-tion, at some point even the most oblivious teenager today might ask a question about the area known as the township of Bath, Summit County, Ohio. They might switch out of music mode to ask, "Is this where LeBron lives?"

Ira Road is one of only five places in the 22.4-mile Summit County section where the towpath trail is interrupted by a vehicular roadway. The many times I crossed Ira Road while riding my bike in the three years I had lived in Akron, I always looked to the left as if I could somehow see five miles down the road to the entrance to camp. This time I simply turned left.

After the dreamy lassitude of the flat towpath trail, the climb out of the Cuyahoga river valley begins in a series of furtive turns and twists. But the effort pays off in a burst of open sky and flat terrain—the vision of a fertile place, an idealized children's book landscape of the perfect farm. The road still seems to respond to an invisible geography, taking bends and curves that respond to lost obstacles. Hills range around this pocket valley in a wreath of raggedy green. After the staccato bursts of steep climbs, the open wash of plowed fields drew me effortlessly in flow.

An old cemetery marks the unlikely corner of Ira and Ira; the road takes a ninety-degree turn, keeping its identity on the perpendicular. One is forced to stop to make the turn to pick which Ira is the right choice. It was a perfect spot to pause before the last few miles to camp. Though I was curious about what the cemetery could tell me, I was more immersed in my own history as I meandered through the old headstones. As I meditated my way around the graves, I was delighted by the density of history at this terminus of Ira. Here and ahead of me was another layer, a fresh way to reclaim the past, to make it new. I had the agency to enter my past unbound by my past.

I leaned against a monument directly centered on the road ahead and scanned the valley. Not far off was Hale Homestead, a destination that was annually dangled before us in grade school as a field trip if we behaved. The photographs were intriguing—bonneted women and suspendered men engaged in farm tasks. We never met the standard for conduct to get there. I was so close to Hale Homestead now, and I felt like I could reach my hand directly from my fifth-grade desk and touch the butter churn. I laughed at the memory, at the strange power in my body.

Directly in front of me, Ira disappeared in an arc of trees across a landscape of topsoil so densely fertile, it smoked, rippling waves of heat-distorted air in rhythms of the late August cicadas. Draining my water bottle, I got back on the bicycle, the last few miles of the pilgrimage on the artery of emotional memory.

In the last section of the approach, I kept my eyes ahead as much as possible. What had been fields and farms on the right had blossomed into theatrically named subdivisions. On the left side of Ira, the Firestone fox grounds were still bordered by white fence, still projecting an air of first estate nobility, for whatever new purpose they now enclosed.

I crossed into the terrain of a past that no longer gripped me, confused me, and motivated me to stand out. Only a slight crunch of gravel under my wheels heralded the triumph. Sun still blazing at five p.m., I parked and headed directly for the lake. I needed a swim.

On the beach I once guarded, a cluster of white heads gathered around a whirring blender. I recognized a few people. Many, most, seemed to know me and knew that I arrived by bicycle. Most, all, it seemed, joined in discussing who would take me home in their car. I wondered if I seemed travel weary, in need of assistance, and why they were vying for my delivery home when I had only just arrived. Their conversation seemed to be about me, not to me. I did not know what to say. I asked where I could change for a swim.

Over the whir of a rigged-up blender churning margaritas, someone shouted, "Use cabin four—it's where our stuff is."

I was already uncomfortable.

In cabin four, I saw that I had woefully under packed for an overnight. This was camp—the simple bunk beds held plastic covered foam mattresses only. I brought not so much as a hand towel. Already I needed to ask for something, already a reason to feel bad.

They were still talking about my transport home when I got back to the beach, including offering to do so before dark. Their voices competed with the whirling blender producing a fresh set of cocktails on its rickety stand amidst the beach chairs. I wondered if they forgot they had invited me to stay the night.

Someone asked me to play a round of cornhole.

"How about after my swim?" seemed a normal response, and thus accepted. I wondered if I had heat stroke; I felt so disconnected.

I stood about for a moment, not really able to enter any of the conversations. It seemed they were enjoying their own rituals of camp as adults. Away from home on safe grounds, it was after five and the bar was open. These were people I should be able to talk to, but they were in another rhythm, not one I could find entry. I was having a hard time hearing and understanding what anyone was even talking about.

Attempting to appear casual, I took a red licorice rope out of a container, something to do.

"Oh, help yourself," said a voice at the table, someone I did not know—and had no idea if she was being satirical. But it was too late to put it back

in the container. Its red plastic texture and taste felt just right for my diminishing sense of presence. A suffocating wave threatened me, high and dark.

"A swim will fix me up," I mumbled and gave myself direction.

I dove into that particular green of Northeast Ohio fresh water, opened
my eyes to its cool swish and turned over under the surface to look through
to the blue sky. I love to swim and will do so in just about any old body of
water. As an adult, I acquired an allergy to fresh water, or maybe to the
things that prosper in fresh water. I decided that having a runny nose and
weepy eyes might be just fine and dove deep with my eyes open.

It was lovely and fine as I swam across toward the giant willow trees
that are long gone, their sturdy overhanging limbs no longer shading the
lake. There was one massive trunk that sloped at the right angle to climb
up and along to the rope swing that Sam, myself, and others of a certain
kind of bravado would swing from, summersaulting in air and down through
the surface of the lake.

And it's okay that the trees were gone. I live in the present now. The
lake, the layered water, warm on top and, degreeing cool as I dove down,
restored the strain of the hot ride. The water feels the same.

I turned back to the beach.

The white heads were tiny against the surprise of the view beyond that
group, a view unchanged in the forty years since I last swam in the lake. The
red buildings crouched against the stone ledges rising behind them. The
tops of the trees at the tops of those ledges towered over me, a dot out in
the lake. It was lovely and clarifying. That was the feeling I wanted, not to
try to make a new memory.

I came out of the water renewed on every level. I lay on the dock in the
sun to dry, the conversation in the shade was sweet incomprehensible buzz.
The metal dock made those same chirpy friction sounds. I fought the desire
to sleep, just hovering in the dreamy nothing of warmth and panting breath.

After my skin dried, I rose, walked to cabin four, dressed, and went
straight to my bicycle without saying a word to anyone. There was nothing
wrong with those white heads except that Sam's was not among them. I
would explain later, and they would understand. I would just say it was too
much for me. They all knew what camp had been once, but they found a
different way to keep it. For me, I wanted it as I knew it then. I had an adult

friend named Sam, but I wanted to keep the child one too. The great thing for me was that I could manage it. I had ridden thirty-six miles for a swim. I flew up Ira Road in a time machine. The ride back was the real journey that day; free from the need of any preserving ritual, hair wet, my own agency, and no stops to home.

II

The Holy See

With cars flying past, a pedestrian walking from St. Thomas Hospital
toward downtown Akron on the Y Bridges feels a sudden lift, a curi-
ous floating away from solid ground, air under feet. Looking down,
the sudden extreme depth comes as a shock of the ordinary. After a
moment, the eye adjusts to the avian perspective. Perched above the
roofs and quaint tidy street plan of Cascade Village, time, sound and
space are slightly unhinged. Though the Little Cuyahoga River runs
white over its rocky bed, the accompanying sound is not the water but
the beating rhythmic hum of tires on air.

In 1935, St. Thomas Hospital in Akron, Ohio had a chronic shortage of
available beds for patients. For some two decades prior, Akron experienced
a shortage of beds. The boom years of the rubber industry brought massive
numbers of men out of the mines of West Virginia to the rubber factories
of Akron. The demand for housing far exceeded the existing capacity, so
the families stayed in the hill towns while the men shared shifts in the factory
and shifts in the beds of rooming houses in South Akron.

In 1935, though the number of factories had declined since the peak
production years of the decade between 1910 and 1920, there were still 132
rubber companies in Akron. The boom years were over, and throughout

the thirties, the sheer numbers of semiskilled labor in a one-industry town found its power in long—at times violent—efforts to form an effective international union.

It was the Great Depression, a decade of vast shortages of material needs and a profusion of zeal to offset the desperation of those needs. In Akron, such zeal added to the increasing numbers of white Evangelicals responding to the simple redemptive messages of Baptist preacher Dallas F. Billington. He created one of the first industrial-scale churches in America, the Akron Baptist Temple. The outsized serious man of compassion was also blessed with a keen sense of marketing, recognizing the potential of radio to reach beyond the local troubled souls of Akron's blue collars.

The passion of working men finding a new power of their own was one answer to the worldwide spiritual malaise of the 1930s. Another could always be found in the stretch of taverns and hotels lining the route between the Summit Lake neighborhood and Firestone Rubber complex along South Main Street.

St. Thomas Hospital in the mid-1930s reflected the emotions of the city it served. With a waiting list for beds, doctors came to the admitting office themselves to appeal for spots for their patients. The admitting administrator, Sister Ignatia, knew the disposition of every bed in the hospital. Frail and slight, she had a wealth of qualities suited to assuage the egos of doctors accustomed to having their demands met. Her personal charm, wit, and compassion kept things light as she maintained the inadequate bed count.

Before Dr. Robert H. Smith came into her office in August 1939, Sister Ignatia had found ways on her own to shelter those suffering from the effects of chronic alcoholism. In this, she was acting in defiance of not just her own hospital, but hospitals generally. Unless an active alcoholic had a medical condition requiring treatment, hospitals had no means of accommodating such patients. They were to be avoided because their problems were not medically treatable, they often exhibited violent behavior, and frequently were unable to pay their hospital bills.

When she could, Sister Ignatia would find some spot for a drunk to have at least a few hours of sleep in a corridor or closet of St. Thomas. Frequently, however, her unorthodox admittees caused trouble. Though they might be sincere when promising her they would be quiet, a drunk with extreme withdrawal symptoms could be out of control. Just before Dr. Smith came to her office, a man she admitted to the general medical services ward kept the night supervisor busy throughout her entire shift.

By the time the doctor approached Sister Ignatia, an as-yet-unnamed movement was keeping some alcoholics sober. Since they had first met in Akron three years earlier, the doctor and his partner Bill Wilson thought they had a solution for the incurable dipsomaniac. They knew from their own experience that it was possible to stop drinking. The two men stayed sober by talking to each other. Before this simple solution had a chance with an active alcoholic, a candidate for the cure needed to be clear of the immediate effects of alcohol poisoning with a safe place to dry out.

Dr. Bob came to Sister Ignatia frustrated and discouraged. It was a tough year for their new idea. He could not persuade Akron City Hospital to reconsider admitting alcoholics, despite his promises to supervise them. In New York, his partner Bill was suffering from another bout of manic depression. Though the two men knew they had something to offer, they also recognized the need for something they could not offer—medical care for the alcoholic. They just needed a bed.

Many of the Akron men who were now sober as a result of the three-year experiment in fellowship had mentioned Sister Ignatia to Dr. Smith. When they had been laid low by their alcoholic obsession, they remembered St. Thomas as a haven, thanks to her kindness in tending their shattered nerves.

The tall discouraged doctor and the frail sister talked for a long time that day. They discovered they had far more in common than it might appear. They knew something essential that was not recognized in medicine or cultural norms. Though its symptoms were aggressively physical, they shared the unique idea that alcoholism was a spiritual malady.

In the office that day, their individual experience of hopelessness gave them the visceral understanding of the cure for a condition of hopelessness. Whether they actually spoke of their experiences—for the doctor, alcoholism and for the nun, nervous breakdown—both knew that only through surrender to a powerful, vital life force, a god of one's own understanding, could a shattered human being be restored.

With the doctor's assurances that the patient would be no trouble, she agreed to take his patient. After the night passed without incident, the doctor came down to see her, asking if the patient could be moved to a private room. There would be visitors coming to see him, and privacy for their conversation was vitally important.

Despite the bed shortage, she told him she would do what she could. There were no private rooms, but after she determined that a bed could fit through the door of the flower-arranging room, she had the patient moved there.

From that first mutually supported alcoholic patient in 1939 until he died in 1950, Dr. Robert Smith, familiar to alcoholics worldwide as Dr. Bob, treated 4,800 patients. St. Thomas Hospital in Akron, Ohio, became the first hospital to officially adopt a permanent policy that recognized the rights of alcoholics to receive hospital treatment.

After establishing the ward at St. Thomas Hospital in Akron, Sister Ignatia was reassigned by her order, the Sisters of Charity of St. Augustine, to an expanding hospital in Cleveland. The hospital wanted to open the first facility specifically designed for treating alcoholics. Based on her experiment with Dr. Bob at St. Thomas, she drew a sketch of how the ward should function. She ran the Rosary Hall Solarium at St. Vincent Charity Hospital in Cleveland, Ohio, until her frail physical condition led to her retirement in 1966.

As Bill Wilson wrote in her memory,

> Never before or since those early Akron days have we witnessed a more perfect synthesis of all these healing forces: Dr. Bob exemplified both medicine and AA; Sister Ignatia and the Sisters of Charity of Saint Augustine also practiced applied medicine; and their practice was supremely well animated by the wonderful spirit of their Community. A more perfect blending of Grace and talent cannot be imagined.

A series of courageous decisions made in Akron created what became known as Alcoholics Anonymous. Around half a century later, what happened in Akron back then saved my life for the second time.

Creation Groans

In the large open space of the Front Porch Café on Grant Street in Akron, Ohio, it was breakfast as usual. Eggs, bacon, and ham sizzled on the grill. Customers spread out among the sixteen tables, arms propped on the blue and white checked plastic covers. A young intern carried a carafe of hot coffee, refilling ceramic mugs. Regulars might have noticed that Joe Tucker, the executive director, was not parked at his spot, the back corner table, just outside the tiny office. Nor was Head Chef Thomas Jones flipping eggs at the grill. The building manager Eric Harmon was not around. Amber Cullen, communications director, who on most mornings disappeared behind her laptop in the middle table on the south wall, really had disappeared that morning. Gary, the assistant chef, was the only staff member in the room. Everyone else working in the café that morning was a volunteer.

The staff was in the back room.

Having a back room to be in was a monumental achievement for the organization, a small urban Christian ministry. Throughout the seven years preceding their assembly in the renovated space that day, the back room had been a neglected nuisance. It was a cold, dismal collection of donated and discarded objects. Co-founder Duane Crabbs was open to all kinds of ideas of what the place could be, and the back room contained a museum of his unrealized visions. The roof was forever leaking somewhere, prompting the

staff to move greasy stacks of bulky industrial kitchen equipment from one
spot to another.

There was nothing outwardly unusual about the group gathered in the
back room drinking coffee and catching up. That ordinariness is what made
it so extraordinary. Such casual normalcy was a major milestone, a stark
indication of growth; they were more than a one-room shop. For the seven
years South Street Ministries owned the building, the front room was the
whole show.

The front room was a full-service breakfast and lunch restaurant with
a lot of off-menu options. The undivided space of the front room created
a physical transparency for the ministry—everything happened in that
space, often simultaneously. It operated as a dining room, town hall, drop-in
center, office and meeting space, performance hall, party center, message
board, and twelve-step recovery room. With the renovation of the back
room and the second floor, they tripled their operating space. Now they
had to figure out what to do with it.

~

I met the building on my second trip to Akron, the day before my Peace
Corps friend Anne was getting married. In a gesture of optimistic generosity—considering it was the day before his wedding—her fiancé Eric offered
to show me the urban restoration work he did with South Street Ministries.
At least, that was my understanding of the trip to Akron, as I described it
to my sister and my girlfriend as we drove from Cleveland. "The ministry
was given a building. We'll have breakfast in the café they just opened there
before we go on the tour."

Even as I said this, I had a feeling it might not be as straightforward as
it sounded.

This was their first summer of operation for the ministry's restaurant,
the outdoor kitchen phase. I suspected it might be an experience in alternate
dining.

We pulled into the parking lot of the café on a Friday morning in
midsummer July 2011. In the relative safety of the parked car, we watched
as a wild-haired white man holding a spatula in one hand and a cigarette
in the other, jumped around the also smoking grill. That was enough

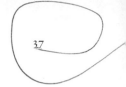

adventure already for my companions, but we had come this far and were expected inside.

I bolstered the courage of my companions while knowing that my girlfriend was already composing the story for the benefit of our friends back in New York. We opened the car doors and stepped out.

Freddie introduced himself, his white hair standing on end behind the red bandana framing his creased tanned face. He waved his spatula as though trying to dismiss the vision of three additional customers. As the ambassador to the dubious twosome behind me, I was all the more exuberant as we pierced the gauntlet of smoke and fire from the grill and from Freddie.

The breakfast that followed was a triumph of performance art over dining, a rhythm of eggs and toast arriving every ten minutes or so.

I was attuned. Akron had produced a sound I recognized somewhere in the fluency of my language of space. The divining rod of my own body indicated treasure in the soil. I paid attention. During the endless breakfast, Eric, understandably distracted about going from a bachelor to a married man in less than twenty-four hours, passed us to the care of Tom Fuller, a successful businessman and friend of the ministry.

Tom showed us the building first. Upstairs, in what had been a single-room occupancy hotel, Joe Heindel had claimed a room for his luthier shop. Despite my suspicions that he was often interrupted by the curious, you would think the guy had nothing else to do but show his beautiful hand-crafted stringed instruments. He remembered our visit well. "My wife just called me before you came in. She told me she was pregnant. I saw you right after I found out we were having our first child, our Frankie."

Tom's next stop was Duane and Lisa Crabbs' house. Tom explained that they had moved to the neighborhood of South Akron based on a calling to serve the inner city. For the fifteen years since starting South Street Ministries, they had raised their children and the organization from the house, a solid foursquare farmhouse. We stood in the driveway—I do not remember the reason why we did not meet them, because I was already drawn to something else. Aside from the initial unease when one first encounters what seems like a "bad area," I was aware of an energy coming through my feet. The house was no different than the houses around it, aside from the half-basketball court immediately to the front of the house and the dominance of its site atop the highest hill in the area. There was the steady hum of the nearby freeway, the one that sliced through Akron, dividing it north and south. As I stood in that driveway, looking at that house, voices blurred and faded for a moment. Something connected me to the ground, as though my feet had sprouted roots.

Where the veil between the known and unknown lifts for a moment, we get a brief look at the other side. This is a phenomenon understood in native and Celtic traditions, spirituality of place, of the physical mystic encounter with something greater than self. We think of such places as somewhere in the wilderness, the desert, the woods. They can happen anywhere. They happen on boiling days in July, standing in a driveway of an old foursquare farmhouse on a hill on a mysterious morning of elliptical sightseeing in Akron.

There was that tug on the sleeve, the roots shooting into the earth from my feet. The deepest part of the earth held them, as though I could sway in a full arc around them, like the Tin Man in the *Wizard of Oz* and stay upright, firm, and fast. I only noticed it, mysterious in coming, mysterious in going. The indistinct sounds of my companions came back to the comprehensible. No one else in the group seemed affected. So I just stayed quiet and got back in the car, reasonably assured that I was outwardly the same to everyone.

The hills of Akron are a string of such places, edgy urban thin spots.

This spiritual bookmark was placed in the middle of my engaged life.

Already overwhelmed by the driveway moment, as we drove through downtown, we passed the Mayflower Hotel. This spot is the spring of Alcoholics Anonymous and the worldwide twelve-step recovery movement. I was astonished at its living presence on Main Street. Though it had seen better days, Art Deco details above the rough ground floor presence gave it a handsome brow. I nodded in its direction and gave a brief benediction of gratitude and acknowledgment for the second instance of Akron saving my life. I returned to New York, not fully aware of how the wedding weekend shook the globe of my Manhattan life.

By any measure, mine was a very good life. I had a ton of great friends. I was working with good clients, sharing office space with other architect friends, teaching a design class at Parsons School of Design, and swimming

every day. A year of dating a wonderful woman grew into living together. But despite all that, I had a persistent restlessness. I had the feeling that it was not my life anymore, or it was not the one I was meant to be living. My restlessness prior to visiting Akron focused on finding a project of worth. I started casting around for something that aligned with my professed social values, with the life I experienced in the Peace Corps. That was not working out well in New York City, and I started looking further afield.

My girlfriend was supportive of the idea of a temporary sojourn.

"Just give me the address where to send the peanut butter."

I wrote to my newly married Peace Corps pal, Anne, to ask her if she knew anything about the Catholic Worker houses in Akron. Yes, she was aware of them, at the same time inviting me to the fifteenth anniversary celebration of South Street Ministries.

"Come see what we are up to," she wrote.

"But they are faith-based!" I immediately thought in horror, as though it were a contagious disease. Then I remembered that I had a spiritual life. I remembered her wedding weekend, the rooted moment in the driveway. The South Street Ministry people seemed to be living the work I claimed to be interested in, not just talking about it. I made plans to come to the anniversary in March.

The weekend of the South Street anniversary, Anne and Eric hosted me in their newlywed home, an apartment over a garage in the Kenmore neighborhood. It lay in close proximity to the lake that I had noticed on my way into the city on the first visit. My enthusiasm for the lake did not seem to be shared by the people living around it. Given Summit Lake's location, geography, age, size, and history, it would seem obvious as the heart of the surrounding neighborhoods, but it was more of a barricade between east and west. The lake seemed nothing more to the locals than a wide wet line between two distinct neighborhoods: Summit Lake and Kenmore. Both areas have similar challenges but different reputations, characterized by their respective drug choices; Summit Lake was the crack side, and Kenmore the meth side.

A vivid example of this description loomed over their apartment. The property on the uphill edge of the street had been destroyed in a meth lab explosion four months prior. The house was locally known as "The Alamo"

for its volatile activity, its anomalous Spanish flat roof style, and its defensive
perch high on the natural ridge running the length of the west side of the
lake. Walking up the steep drive to the scorched but standing stucco remnant
of the house, I noticed an acrid mix of mold and melted plastic clinging to
the place. The view in front of the intriguing ruin was captivating. In front
of the backdrop of the remains of South Akron industry, there was a body
of water, and I was completely enthralled by this natural feature. A reasonable swimmer could cross it five minutes. But it was developed and abused
in such a way that its notoriety carried the negative associations of intractable pollution, crime, and suicide. No one I talked to seemed half as excited
as I was about Summit Lake.

The morning after the anniversary celebration, I was graciously invited
to attend a meeting of the Board of South Street Ministries. Chatting with
Noelle Beck beforehand, we discovered a mutual love of bicycles. Noelle
casually said, "You know you can ride a bicycle from Akron to Cleveland
on a continuous path."

That was it. That was the keystone moment. The keystone is the central,
top stone in any arch. Until the keystone is in place, the two reaching arms
of an arch cannot stand unsupported. When the keystone is placed, it locks
the arch and all the weight and anything passing on top of the arch is conducted safely down.

The flow of weight becomes liquid, as light as a raindrop down a wall,
seeking to return to earth. For me, with that bit of news about the bike path,
I experienced an instant physical change. On some level, I heard a noise,
the grit of stone against stone as the chiseled last bit slid into place between
the two sides of an arch, and the weight of stone became liquid.

I have never made a true arch as an architect. There are more efficient
ways to carry load across an opening today—the strength of industrially
produced or enhanced materials far precludes any thought of using the
revolutionary Roman building technique now. So while as human beings,
we love arches and they continue to appear in our buildings, they are but a
child's rendering of the form—a crude crayon version we applaud and
cherish but is only a line, with no depth. It is a shadow in our human shared
psyche—that bold liberating engineering, the Roman curve that changed
the world forever.

My life moments are remembered as architecture. The epiphanies take shape as space, often accompanied by sound. It snaps my attention to the present moment in a realignment of everything in my body. The keystone was simultaneous with the decision to move to Akron. After the assembly of my own reaching arms upward, heavy, that last central stone found its place in a silent slip of stone dust and the arch was complete. The span was made from there—New York City—to here—Akron, Ohio.

I had grown up only thirty miles from where we sat. Thirty miles I now learned I could cycle back to directly. The arch epiphany exploded my sense of pilgrimage. My perpetual yearning to walk the fourth branch of the medieval Camino de Santiago vanished in the sudden understanding that any path is a pilgrimage, that all roads are sacred.

Blinking and stiff from the impact of Noelle's offhand remark, I held still as the voices and people in the room settled from murky to clear. No one at the table noticed I had disappeared. There it was again, a vanished moment in Akron. I found out later that such moments are encounters with the mystical, the mystery. It is a kind of spiritual seizure, in which everything immediate disappears. I blinked my way back to the present moment as the meeting was about to start. I sat quietly as the meeting opened with a prayer. This was the first time in my life I had ever experienced a business meeting that opened with a prayer. Not that I needed a prayer, having just gotten a direct call.

South Street Ministries was at a point in their story I understood well. Fifteen years is a benchmark for not-for-profit organizations. They either grow or fade at that point. Working as an architect for artistic institutions at similar points, I recognized that I could be of service to my Akron hosts. By the meeting's conclusion, my decision was made. It would be more than a temporary sojourn. I decided to move to Akron.

What I projected to be a commitment of two years took six, but the building was done, and the staff sat in the back room to figure out what came next.

The only thing that was the same about the back room was its name. By function, it was now a community health clinic run by Faithful Servants, a Christian-based healthcare organization founded by two married doctors, Susan and Mark Meyers. In medical school, they were inspired by a doctor who moved to rural Mississippi to work alongside John Perkins, a man who also deeply influenced Duane Crabbs' decisions. The clinic is a flexible space, and by all appearances that morning, it was a place of assembly for exactly the purpose of their gathering: planning the future.

I stood with two South Street board members and three invited guests awaiting the start of three days of strategic planning. Donovan Harris, Eric Nelson, and I had been included as invested friends of South Street. My official role as architect was almost complete, but my relationship with South Street was beyond a bound set of construction documents.

The two women conducting the seminar arranged the typical tools for such sessions: the white board, flip charts, thousands of colored markers, and a vast assortment of sticky notes. Their personal equipment was minimal, reduced to the two essentials of power: the palm-sized device containing a PowerPoint presentation and the enormous personalized plastic vessel of colored water. They were facilitators trained in a procedure intimidatingly titled "StratOps."

Conspicuously absent in the mix was co-founder Duane Crabbs. By loose mutual agreement with the Executive Director Joe Tucker, Duane would participate as called in. Duane's wife Lisa, the co-founder of the ministry, was in the room. Though she had no responsibility that morning beyond her presence, she was busy around the refreshment table. Her lifetime habits meant making sure there was enough of everything to eat and drink before the meeting started.

Duane and Lisa Crabbs are the grace and glue of the ministry; he, the fluid energetic grace to her steady, enduring glue. The light shines on Duane but shadow or sun, rain, or sleet, it is Lisa who holds the whole thing together. Twenty years had passed since they started the ministry after moving into the Summit Lake neighborhood. Without a plan or training, they operated on abundant faith and sometimes less abundant hope. It was a commitment to fidelity; they responded to the call of the heart for service through the example of Jesus.

In the twenty years since they started South Street Ministries, the organization had evolved into a more formal structure. The concrete chunk of a twenty-year anniversary presented the space and opportunity to recognize the need for future planning. It was a good moment for standing still in the new space of the clinic and taking notes for the next phase.

To the world around the café, South Street Ministries and Duane Crabbs were synonymous. However, functionally and fundamentally the ministry had moved away from the charismatic singularity of Duane. Even those in the community did not know that for over five years Duane had no official role or authority over decisions made by the ministry he founded.

For any organization, moving beyond the identity of the founder is a difficult journey. A future at South Street without the everyday charisma of Duane and Lisa was not a vision for most to entertain. For the stability of the ministry, Joe and the board decided there was no reason to delay that inevitability.

The hiring of outside strategic planning consultants often constitutes a warning flag, a sign of trouble akin to marriage counseling for corporations. However, South Street ran in continuous laps of crisis management, so a kind of chaos was normal for everyone present. Moreover, the "outside consultants" in this situation were more like family.

If anything, the organization had never been more stable. There was no confusion about the mission, no crisis in leadership, no subterfuge in the ranks. They were in the enviable situation of a focused pause after the completion of impressive benchmarks for a ministry of their size. It was less breakdown than breakthrough. It was a time to glance back and then forward together, a luxury unknown in their day-to-day operation, their triage-style life.

It was Thomas, the café manager, who pointed out something no one else in the room noticed.

"Look, we're all in here, and the café is working fine without us."

Though that level of daily functionality had been common for quite a while, being together in the back room let us all take it in with some detachment.

～

We settled into the prepared half-circle of chairs. The last active use of the back room space had been as the bar of the Croatian American Club. It was the only part of the building in use by the time the Croatians closed it down in 2005. Now, the only remnant of those days was something I loved including on my tours of the building. Inside the enormous wooden walk-in cooler, the plaster walls were frescoed with its working man's past; in black letters, the words "Pabst," "Iron City," "Schlitz" were preserved in the damp chill.

Before the renovation, J. T. Buck, a musician who grew up in the neighborhood, knew the exact spot of his father's bar stool. Pointing to the debris-strewn concrete floor, the curved footprint of the bar was still visible.

"Right there, every afternoon," J. T. said as he moved his finger energetically towards the floor, "that was his spot."

The arrangement of folding chairs curved over neutral mixed gray carpet tiles. Glass block had replaced the plywood and broken window frames. Fresh, simple, clean, new, and reassuringly anonymous, the back-room clinic completely eradicated the perpetual dinge of its prior lives.

StratOps co-facilitator Noelle Beck got things started. It was Noelle's offhand remark about a bike path to Cleveland that tipped my decision to move to Akron. She and her husband Tim had created a teen center in Kenmore. First Glance grew from borrowed space in a local church to three connected commercial buildings on Kenmore Boulevard. Bonded in their Evangelical Christian faith, Noelle and Duane diverged completely in their sense of organizational life. Noelle managed the complex and ever-expanding outreach for teens with disarming ease and inscrutable calm. StratOps facilitator is Noelle's latest credential in her prodigious capacity as a leader and planner.

After starting with prayer, Noelle and her partner Alicia asked us to introduce ourselves and identify our positions. It's an open secret at South Street that no one is actually qualified for his or her job. If the decision to hire any one of them relied on paper credentials, the room would be empty. However, in the grounding of faith and the instincts of Duane, it had worked in that manner for twenty years. The sturdy alchemy of the mission statement was obvious by the mix of those in the room: "Unlikely partners taking shared risks to renew our community for Christ's sake." In the recognition of their mutual brokenness, South Street contained the same power as the twelve-step recovery meetings they hosted. Any wreckage of personal past was not a source of shame, but of strength.

Duane lacked both a degree from a conventional divinity school and ordination by any established religion. However, his intelligence and conviction with people endowed him with an authority. His capacity to recognize and empower potential in those whom the world had dismissed was the Human Resources philosophy of South Street, expressed in a shortened version of the mission statement: "Unlikely partners for Chrissss' sake!"

They did the best they could at the job they had, and it just kept working out. At the Front Porch Café, the primary offering was love, so if efficiency and consistency suffered as a result, no one really seemed to mind.

Noelle gestured to Bobby Irwin, seated at one end or the open curve around her, to start the introductions.

"Hey, I'm Bobby, and I run the After School Program and summer camp."

If asked to identify "Youth Director" from a lineup of twenty random people, Bobby Irwin might be the least likely pick. Bob is a big guy—a really big guy. His face is framed by a red scraggly beard and a bald head. Tattoos run along his strong arms. Fear would be a reasonable reaction if he came your way. But he moves with an even steady country boy rhythm and operates from steadfast fidelity to his faith. Bobby knows what it is like to struggle, because at thirty-six, everything for him has been a struggle. He shifts his feet and controls a stutter when nervous. He understands intimately what hell kids can go through, because he grew up on the same streets they did. He is solid. He loves kids who can be very hard to love, and he does it without ceremony every day.

Erin Woodson is next in the circle. She and Bobby recently announced their engagement. Erin Woodson, like everyone else at South Street, started as a volunteer. As such, she navigated the mechanics of South Street's first big signature fundraiser, Rails 'N' Trails, successfully. She has a master of social work degree, but her position is development director.

Chef Thomas Jones had never worked in a kitchen before he started as assistant chef in the café. Communications Director Amber Cullen, after serving with Mission Year post college, was in her first paid full-time job with South Street. She came up with her own job title.

Job Placement Director Toni Code worked at more jobs in her lifetime than everyone put together in the room that day. Her credentials were direct experience, quick feet, passion and lived understanding for her clients, and the street-smart intolerance of the con.

Joe Tucker has been the executive director for over three years, but until very recently derived most of his income as a math instructor.

Lisa Crabbs and Eric Harmon sat next to each other, as they often did at staff meetings. They shared the same humor that escaped the rest of the staff. Today, the space between their chairs was the seam, the margin between past and future. The foundational years were over. South Street grew by staying in the often-uncomfortable place of the margin, of the uncertainty of "next." Lisa was that—the foundational years, the past. Thirty-six-year-old Eric represented the more classifiable future. He was recently ordained as an Anglican priest after completing a master of divinity degree at Walsh College.

Eric introduced himself in the simple naming of his compound job titles—building and construction project manager and reentry program coordinator.

Lisa's self-identification was by far the shortest of all:

"I do some admin work for the staff."

A mastery of understatement, after a brief pause came the burst of laughter. Lisa's succinct distillation of her role conveyed the steady power behind her impulsive dreamer husband, Duane.

The introductions conveyed something about the nature of the ministry and Duane's empowerment. Everyone at South Street started as a volunteer, learning through the daily experience of the job, whether it was flipping a burger, driving a van of children to a program, tutoring after school, coaching football, or writing newsletters.

The ministry had the idiosyncratic qualities of a family business mixed with the careening operational structure of a support group, maintained by a reliance on God to get through the messy mystery of serving the people who came their way. They did not keep score, and there was no membership list. In the twenty years of its existence, there was never a problem or issue larger than one they could solve themselves.

In the suspended space between the formal strategic plan and the platform of the twenty-year history, there was a definite cultural shift. The prior narrative was immeasurable and improvisational. It had the rhythm and suspense of a juggler adding more objects to the spinning collection already airborne. Sometimes it seemed to prosper in spite of itself and the obstacles of Duane's quixotic leadership. That energy had transformed as the building transformed. Now the building met the standards of occupancy. The ministry's future, its spiritual energetic transformation was not as easy to read as the building.

The StratOps workshop employed a set of tools and techniques well established in American corporate culture. Noelle Beck had an ease with that language to match the ease with the people sitting in the circle around her. The group was equally relaxed. Noelle was a friend.

Introductions complete and overall schedule for the next three days described, it was time to understand the history, the "where we have come from" narrative. Duane was the voice; he would have been the person to tell that story. However, he was not there. Lisa was.

It was never her inclination to speak in public about what she and Duane had brought forth. Nor was it her nature to be reflective. She was the practical half of the marriage, of the partnership. She is a master of constancy. Throughout their original urban adventure, her attention to the detail and capacity to keep things afloat seemed effortless. Lisa was an artist of anonymous management. However, it would be a mistake to interpret her public meekness as an indication of a Christian wife sublimating herself to the husband. She simply aimed her voice where it would be most effective. Though her influence and power were in the background, they were always there, thoughtful, without flourish or intellectualizing a situation. However, Lisa operated on a kind of contradiction also; the paradox of faith opposite her practical management—an absolute trust in God's hand in all things.

Her mind was sharp and clear as a sheet in a ledger book, but now she was laying out an original composition. This was a story everyone in the room thought they already knew. Without the purpose-driven message of her pastor husband, Lisa shared a new history of the ministry's early years and growth.

"We just did the next thing. Everything happened in our house for…years. And in the whole house. Tutoring? Duane's Mom. She was a kindergarten teacher. She just gathered the little kids and took them down to the basement to help them with learning. Duane's parents were our first volunteers. They helped us through so many things."

She paused.

"We needed them. They, well, like everyone else, thought we were making a mistake moving to South Street. But they didn't talk about it, they were there for us, right there. It was hard to take all the negativity, we felt so alone. Everyone told us it was a terrible idea. "What about your kids?"

We just got started. We had a weekly Bible Study in the living room. That went on every Wednesday for years. The Murrays were starting Catholic Worker on Princeton Street then—they came to the Bible Study. Their son Liam, he was one of the people who started Bike shop.

On Thursday nights, we had church in the living room. During the day, the kids, our kids, would be in school there, in the living room. I was teaching them but there were always other kids too, always. Years of kids—in the basement with more volunteers as tutors. We started to partner with Lincoln School to have kids come directly from there to our house."

Lisa paused. In her understated, practical, deadpan, with everyone in the palm of her hand:

"Sometimes I thought Lincoln School sent their worst kids to our house for tutoring.

"It seemed that the worse the neighborhood got, the more we...grew. We would try a lot of different things, whatever seemed like it might help someone. Our yard was open, and with our four kids, it was the center of a lot of games. Anyone could cross from Bachtel through our yard. And I mean anyone. But the neighborhood kids knew they could play there safely. A lot of times it was hard to tell if they were playing or fighting. We put in the basketball court in front of the house. There was always a swing set in the back for the little kids. Our kids had a lot of friends; there were so many kids around, flowing all over the place.

"There were so many different people, so many, who helped us, came alongside us. Our mailman, right after we moved in, helped with carpentry and joined the Bible study. Duane's Cuyahoga Falls firefighter friends built the stairways to the apartment over the garage. That became the Upper Room. We moved the tutoring and After School program into the Upper Room, and that allowed those programs to grow.

"Bike shop really got going, out of our garage twice a week in the summer. People would try different things; the gardening program was one that grew.

"I was home all the time when the kids were growing up. With Duane's work and his ministry in the neighborhood, it was like we were in two separate worlds in those years. He would be out in the neighborhood at night. The phone could ring in the middle of the night, someone needing help.

"There were nights I would be making coffee at three in the morning for a friend in crisis sitting at our kitchen table. I just made sure we always had enough to include someone who might show up.

"Our kids were my big worry before we moved there, but they were fine. They had lots of friends, and we included their friends in our life, in the house. Our kids experienced the sadness and pain of things happening to their neighborhood friends. So many moved away suddenly, without any word. We had to explain why their friends left without saying goodbye.

"A lot of times, most of the time for years, we had someone staying with us, on the living room couch or out on the porch. They were uncles to our kids. Derek Foster and Patrick Armour. Patrick was with us for a long time. And all that time I was doing the bookkeeping, too. From that same desk, the desk in the den.

"We just prayed about whatever was a worry. And the doors just kept opening. A lot of times I was juggling the money we had, spreading it out to keep things running. We prayed. And then something would happen, the money would … come in and we kept going. We just took the next step that God was leading us to."

There was a silence after Lisa finished—a long mutual silence. Even those who knew the story heard a new story, because Lisa had never told it before. She told the story from the center, from the place that for twenty years, people knew they could come and knock and be heard.

The silence, stillness was another reminder that as we sat in the chairs, we also gathered at an intersection. There would be pauses in the next three days, but something beyond the flip-chartable steps and action plans hung in the space. It was Lisa, the unrehearsed beauty of her story, her fidelity, and truth.

~

Noelle and Alicia introduced the next activity, the "Visioning" section. What next? The language around this huge crossroads was a kind of familiar corporate speak. It allowed for a swerve away from what none of us wanted to face yet. The group found a way to talk about the future by the mutual recognition that the DNA of South Street Ministries was Duane Crabbs. That felt like a home base, a comforting solid. It kept the unspoken future at bay for a few more hours of charts and graphs.

Duane came in the late afternoon. He had been in a depression for a few months by then. It happened from time to time with him. His gloom contrasted with the bouncy reassurance of StratOps. His light that normally shone out on the world was draped in felt. Duane was present, but it was hard to tell where he was, really. The conversation wreathed around him, about him. He seemed a wisp of himself, but he was with people who knew and loved all of him, the whole of him. There was no pressure for him to be anything other than what he was in that moment.

The facilitators brought up the next section of the plan. They were poised with their markers to write a list below the heading "Risks to the Ministry." They asked for potential risks.

"Loss of founder identity," someone offered.

It was time. We all needed to take that in.

At some point in the future, Duane would not preach on Sunday. Lisa would not make sure that the necessary details happened or add the unnecessary touches of daily hospitality that graced the café. They would simply not be there. Duane and Lisa had already gone beyond their original commitment of twenty years. Their lives were here, they were not going anywhere. But the day would come when Duane and Lisa would never walk through the door of the café again. South Street had to prepare for that idea—the permanent absence of the singularity of Duane and Lisa Crabbs.

We moved on to the conventions of planning. Lists drawn up, options and outcomes discussed and pie-charted, the white flip chart paper arranged around the room as we completed a new task. We took snack and lunch breaks, laughed, enjoyed the loose captive comradery of our time together. It felt like jury duty with friends and family. By the end of the time, Noelle and Alicia had good words for us, taking down the sheets that lined the entire room and several of the space dividers of the health clinic.

Eventually they would put together the results in a bound copy. Eventually it would sit on a shelf in the tiny office off the café.

A Bed in Sheol

Sheol is the Old Testament Hebrew word for the unseen world of the
dead where departed spirits go. It was a place of stillness and darkness,
but without judgment of moral character. All the dead—righteous
and wicked alike—become shades, without personality or strength.
Sheol is the great equalizer.

The Sunday before Thanksgiving, 2017 at two p.m., Duane and Lisa Crabbs
were in their bedroom, dressing for a family outing. Waiting downstairs
were their two sons. After protesting about the timing of the annual family
photograph session, Josh and Jonathan were the only ones ready on time.

Their oldest, Joshua, was particularly annoyed.

"Who schedules a picture in the middle of Sunday afternoon football?
Can't we just take it in the backyard?"

He and his wife Allie were in their final days in the United States. After
a month-long visit and the birth of their newborn son, they were returning
to their life as missionaries in the Dominican Republic as a new family of
three.

With the three-generation Crabbs family numbering eleven, Sunday
was the only time that worked for an outdoor photograph. The plan was
to gather at their parents' house, the home they all grew up in, to caravan
to the Cleveland Art Museum.

Duane and Lisa heard their two sons laughing about the shirts. They ridiculed each other about who looked worse in the identical shirts they wore, also sported in miniature on Josh's baby son. The shirts were a kind of joke tradition that had developed over the years around getting their picture taken. In the spotless stair hallway, a cascading series of formal studio portraits covered the walls, a study in smiles, bad haircuts, tradition, and love. The staircase documented the family over the twenty-seven years since birth of their first child, Joshua.

Duane sat on the bed, trying to rise above the sudden feeling of extreme weakness. Maybe Josh's burrito from Skeets was a bad idea. The discomfort was impossible to ignore. When he told Lisa he thought he had the flu, she accused him of trying to get out of the plan. She was getting ready in their bathroom and was fed up with the complaints of her men.

"How could you get a flu that fast? You were fine a minute ago downstairs. You are worse than the boys. What game is it you want to watch instead of being with your family?"

He had already put in a full day, up since four a.m. as usual. He habitually rose early, went downstairs, made a thermos of coffee, and sat down amidst several neat stacks of books assembled around his reading chair. That morning he had written and delivered the message at the Front Porch Fellowship Sunday morning church service.

Now, as he tried to overcome the nausea, he heard his boys enjoying their rare time together. It was always great, having the entire family back in the house. It had been over a year since they had been together, for Hannah's wedding. Now there were two new members, Duane and Lisa's first two infant grandsons. The boys called up, impatient, but it was just the family language of routine one-upmanship. It was safe and familiar, a day given over to joy. The bond between the four children was deep and close, forged by the unusual choices their parents made, by their own individual decisions as they matured, and by the unaccountable conditions that create healthy young adults.

Lisa had been looking forward to this day. She had always been the one to insist on a family portrait, but their daughter Hannah had taken charge this time. The simplicity of the day was a welcome change in a long season of loss. The family had just buried her brother's wife. One of their closest friends, Mike Marshall, was recently found in his camper at Put-in-Bay Island, dead, alone, after a massive coronary.

Coming out of the bathroom, she realized immediately that Duane was in trouble. His face was gray and glistening with sweat. Her husband was having a heart attack. In the first wave of shock and panic, she screamed for Joshua and ran downstairs.

Duane, clutching the edge of the bed, shouted back that he was okay. He had no chest pain, and his breath was steady, ruling out a heart attack. But his years as a firefighter and EMS technician told him he was not okay. He recognized his more subtle symptoms signaled some kind of cardiac trouble.

As the boys tried to understand their frantic mother, Duane came down the stairs. Calm and clear, he calculated that it would be faster to simply drive to Akron General than wait for the ambulance. If he called Akron General as he drove there, the emergency staff would be waiting for him. He started out to the car, calling for Josh to bring the car keys and come with him.

Despite the fact that every single person around him was a licensed driver except the two infant grandsons, Duane's intention was to drive himself. Josh had not lived in Akron for over ten years, and all the current work on the expressway had closed off roads Josh might remember. Their house was only a nine-minute drive to Akron General. That Sunday, he knew he could get there in under five minutes, easy. He was steadily reassessing the best and fastest response to the conditions. Such alertness to the environment in threatening conditions was where Duane excelled. But this time he was both victim and emergency responder.

In the few beats between his dad asking for the car keys and finding them, Josh ran out the back door to see his dad face down on the lawn. It was his turn to scream. Duane rose, claiming he was resting. But he did not remember lying down. Meanwhile, Lisa was insisting they use the landline to call 911. Everyone was doing their best to appear and stay calm. Duane, from his involuntary seated view, knew what was happening. He had been in this scene many times, though not in the victim role. His family was starting to panic.

"Josh, you're going to drive. I'll tell you how to get there, son."

~

Exactly one week before, they had all converged for a celebration of Duane and Lisa's twenty-year commitment to serving the neighborhood. The whole family stood together amidst old and new friends in the eclectic community known as the Front Porch Fellowship at the Sunday service. Miller Avenue Church was filled with old and new friends to celebrate the occasion. Duane and Lisa had spent the past year resisting the board's elaborate proposals to honor the twentieth anniversary. They found it perplexing that anyone close to them would suggest anything other than this—a simple worship celebration in the open broad community followed by a meal and fellowship.

The family's journey over those twenty years is studded with characteristic Duane decisions and motivations, perplexing or inspiring to those on the sidelines. Motivated by his desire to engage in his emerging brand of urban ministry full-time, he quit his job as a firefighter, two years shy of his pension eligibility. Whether defiant or foolhardy, for Duane it was a statement of conviction, of the purity of his intent.

In many ways, what was a naturally good fit as a firefighter was not always as successful in matters less urgent than emergency response. Much of who Duane Crabbs became as an influential local leader sprang from his personality bonded to the distinct qualities that make a good firefighter— a public servant willing to face the possibility of injury or death on a daily basis.

A firehouse needs to know that a new guy is a good firefighter, something that cannot be determined until a situation arises on a call. Once the squad knows the new guy has what it takes, unspoken entry is granted to the brotherhood—a brotherhood that also includes relentless ridicule.

When he started his firefighting career in Cuyahoga Falls in 1986, the newbie, the balding guy with the funny name, was deemed okay. He was a good firefighter. Plus Crabbs had a lot of distinct quirks to joke about. He was always reading, didn't play cards, and had funny ideas.

When it counted, it did not take long to realize that Crabbs was the real thing in a crisis. He had what it took, calm and steady, brave and committed to saving lives and protecting his fellow firefighters. Duane had this strange innocence about him, which made the constant joking by his colleagues all the better. He took the teasing well, and he gave it back well.

Still, he learned over time that it was best to keep certain facts of his domestic life on the down low. The firehouse did not need to know about his call to minister in the heart of Akron.

The very qualities that made him a good firefighter might be the opposite of what one seeks in a spiritual counselor. Duane's off-shift profile was extreme to his firefighting brotherhood. While he got the nod as a good firefighter, he was different. He held opinions that were not within the informal recognition of belonging.

Firehouse culture thrives on humor to undercut the inherent danger of the job. Duane suffered through his fair share for being an idealistic do-gooder. While firefighters are typically churchgoing and family-oriented, there is a certain fatalistic humor that comes along with the work. Duane had the competitive alpha-type attitude, but also did not act the tough guy when it came to his Christianity, or his feelings about discrimination.

When he became a Cuyahoga Falls firefighter in 1986, the force was one hundred percent white. It bothered him that there was not one full time African American employee in the city administration, and he did not hesitate to speak out on the issue. Added to his other distinctions, it was another source of fuel for the continuous firehouse badinage. By 1989, though the department had been integrated with the first three Black firefighters, Duane was drawn to work in the place that he had found his ministry.

He wanted to work in the City of Akron. The contradiction of living in Akron, worshipping at a Black church in Summit Lake and then turning away from all that to work outside the city was getting to him. He felt like he was facing the wrong direction, not acting on God's call to serve the inner city.

It would mean that he would be starting all over again, as though the four years in the Falls had never happened. He knew it would mean submitting to testing by another firehouse, getting the worst cleaning jobs in the station, and accepting a new chain of command that would include African American leadership. He knew it would be more dangerous and more work for less pay—a reduction of one third of his current salary.

Lisa, always more cautious in decision-making, had concerns about the salary reduction, but otherwise supported Duane's idea. The couple had chosen to live in a mixed-race neighborhood in Akron. Despite her worries about the reduced household income, her views about money were tempered by growing up in a family that made the best of lean finances and remained close and supportive throughout it all. She was resourceful. Beyond that, it was a simple matter of faith with Lisa. If this is what God was calling Duane to do, then he needed to listen and follow as far as it would take him.

Duane took the first step towards the Akron Fire Department by taking the written test in 1990. He began to tell the guys at work his plans, bragging that Akron was the far more manly option. His colleagues seized on this delicious opportunity to ridicule what they saw as a stupid move. It added to the abundant material they had to tease "Buster," one of Duane's many firehouse handles, after the Olympic gold medalist movie star Buster Crabbe. Nicknames were abundant in the house, and Buster suited Duane particularly well. He was a buster alright.

But a month later, when Duane got the test results, instead of his expectation to be in the top twenty percent, he had failed the test. There was a section on firefighter personality to which he had not given much consideration, thinking it was subjective and therefore not graded. It included the statement, "I would rather read a book than be in a crowded room full of people." Asked to answer honestly, he agreed. It was the wrong answer and the source of his failing mark.

The guys teased him mercilessly for failing to have a firefighter's personality.

"Buster, you didn't have to take a test! We could have told them you don't fit in!"

He found it hard to accept Lisa's suggestion that perhaps it was not God's will. But there was nothing to be done but wait the two years and take the test again to find out what God had in mind. In his disappointment, he decided that the next time he would simply lie and give every aggressive alpha male stereotypical answer.

Fortunately for Duane's planned tweaking of God's will, the personality survey was dropped from the exam when he took it for the second time, two years later in 1992. His score was in the top five percent. He advanced to the next level.

Though Duane's firefighter personality included choosing to read a book over being in a crowded room, he had plenty of alpha male in him. He looked forward to the next test, physical agility. One part of the test involved crawling through a maze in full gear, including the self-contained breathing apparatus known as SCBA. For this test, the face mask is completely blacked out to simulate zero visibility situations. Duane had helped run this test and felt very confident on the testing day. Fire Chief Alexander came by to watch. Duane volunteered to go first. Claiming he would set the fastest time ever recorded, the chief flatly responded

"How 'bout you just pass the test."

Boasting, betting, and challenging are common among firefighters, but it is always behavior, action more than any spoken claim that counts in the squad. Sightless, oxygen mask on his face and full turnout gear, Duane crawled through the maze in three minutes twenty-seven seconds, the fastest time ever posted. He passed the physical exam.

〜

On the day of his heart attack, Duane talked his way through it all until the oxygen mask was placed over his mouth. All the way to the hospital as Josh drove, he talked, guiding Josh along the fastest route. He called the hospital emergency room, utterly calm, describing his own symptoms. By the time they arrived, the hospital staff was ready and immediately got to work. Duane cooperated with the medics' instructions, falling into his custom of connecting with others, reaching out, keeping it easy, talking and smiling his way onto the stretcher.

He kept gesturing after he lay on the stretcher, his smile visible under the oxygen mask. Before he disappeared behind the emergency room double doors, he waved to Lisa.

〜

Passing the physical exam for the Akron Fire Department brought Duane to the next challenge, the psychological test. Duane's results were problematic, and he was asked to take the test again, making sure to consider the questions and answer honestly. Again, the results were red flagged. He was asked to come in for an interview with a psychologist. After probing Duane's beliefs for a half hour, the therapist stopped.

"Only an angel could score as you have. Could you really be that idealistic?"

Duane laughed, said she should talk to his wife or the guys he worked with about that. But he readily admitted that he was idealistic.

"I am trying to come to Akron for one-third less money, and twice the work because I believe that God wants me to work in the city."

In the silence that followed, Duane was aware that the woman before him held his future in the long empty pause. He thought it best to say no more. He prayed into the long space. The psychologist broke the mood with a chuckle, saying she was recommending him for the job.

The next and final test in the process was the medical exam. It was administered only to otherwise-approved candidates. Duane sat in the waiting room of the Morley Health Center, waiting for his name to be called. This was all that stood between him and taking the oath. But he waited, knowing that he was about to take a test that he could not pass—the vision test. The threshold was a minimum 20/60 vision. Duane's uncorrected vision was 20/200. It was a reality he chose to ignore in his quest. His clear conviction of his destiny, his sincere faith that God wanted him to be in the city had carried him this far.

Akron's standard physical was more rigorous than Cuyahoga Falls and was based on the Los Angeles County Fire Department's 1972 standard. However, the vision threshold in the twenty years since that standard had been revised in many departments due to the refinement and increased use of contact lenses. The lenses changed everything regarding firefighter safety. Prior to lenses, even the best candidates without that minimum unassisted visual acuity could not be firefighters. Eyeglasses cannot be worn under the SCBA face mask. The ear stems prevent the mask from a complete seal, allowing toxic smoke to enter the mask, jeopardizing the firefighter's safety, and threating the success of the mission. Contact lenses obviated the handicap. But Akron still used the 1972 standard.

The nurse brought him to the exam room and excused herself for a moment when the phone rang. Duane seized on the opportunity and memorized enough of the lines of the chart to pass. He took the opportunity as his good fortune, God providing him a space to move forward.

The nurse noted his visual acuity at 20/40, a pass. As she applied the blood pressure cuff, Duane was struggling with growing remorse for cheating.

The blood pressure reading prompted the nurse to ask him if he had blood pressure problems in the past.

"Never," he answered, honestly.

Saying it was too high to meet the standard, the nurse prepared the cuff for a second reading as Duane explained that the blood pressure was not a problem, but that he was a Christian, and he had just cheated on the eye exam. She readministered both tests. Blood pressure, pass. Visual acuity, fail.

The rejection letter he received the following week concluded with a slender possibility for Duane's persistent uncorrected vision and a conduit for his God-inspired inner vision: "If you have any questions or wish to contest this decision, you must contact the office of the Civil Service Commission in writing within five days."

Duane wrote immediately to the personnel director of the city of Akron, Richard Pamley, indicating his intention to contest, sending it the same day, certified mail. He had a new idea.

Akron had not made changes in its physical in the twenty years since the LA County standards had been adopted. Many departments, including the Cuyahoga Falls Fire Department incorporated corrective contact lenses into consideration. Even the most recent standard issued by the National Fire Protection Association allowed firefighters to wear contact lenses under their face masks. He felt he had the basis for a solid case. As he waited for his hearing, he kept researching and preparing. He had hope, until he found out how the hearing was conducted.

The Civil Service hearing is composed of three panelists appointed by the mayor. They make their ruling in private and issue the result in writing. Rarely do they overturn in favor of the petitioner and against the city's original decision. The petitioner cannot present the case unless represented by a lawyer.

Duane could not afford an attorney, but he took up his own defense with customary zeal.

Duane and Lisa had befriended the elderly widow in the house behind theirs on Stadelman Street. She was the mother of Akron Fire Captain Roger Hoover. He and Duane had often talked over the fence when Roger cut his mother's grass. Roger encouraged Duane in his campaign, telling him to investigate the records of past hearings.

Duane's subsequent investigation of the records revealed that in the 1990 alone, the vision standard had been protested forty times and upheld. Checking back to 1988, it was protested sixty times. Though it was a discouraging history, Duane continued to polish his presentation. As long as he still had a chance, he was determined to put every effort into the campaign.

Duane's backyard buddy Captain Roger Hoover phoned one day. He had some exciting news for Duane. He overheard several of the assistant chiefs discussing the newly enacted Americans with Disabilities Act. Though not yet adopted into general building codes as they apply to the private sector, the legislation was legally mandated for government entities. The new law dictated that if a person was denied a job based on a physical disability, the burden of proof fell on the employer to show that the disability made the employee unfit for the job. The chiefs expressed concern that the new law would open the city to lawsuits.

Hoover thought Duane's complaint fell into that category. Roger encouraged Duane to contact the city, the fire department, anyone who might be influential in the application of the new federal statute. Now Duane had a second course of action. Hoover advised Duane to continue work on his presentation as the hearing date approached.

Within days of the hearing, Duane received a phone call from the personnel director of the City of Akron, Richard Pamley. He asked Duane if he would provide some details about his complaint over the phone. Duane had no reluctance to respond. In fact, he welcomed the opportunity to present his case early, before the hearing date. Comfortable with the spontaneous opportunity, he was a firefighter blessed by a love and a skill for persuasive speech. All the work he had done allowed him to speak to the authority at the other end of the line with his own calm authority.

By the time he cited the new ADA legislation, Pamley interrupted, asking if Duane would be willing to bring the information to his office. Duane could not have been more eager for such an opportunity—an opportunity he was barred from doing at the actual hearing. He was confident now that a direct presentation of his work would be persuasive. At the very least, it could not hurt the case and would be good practice for any future opportunity.

Duane brought his research and verbal dexterity to Pamley's office. Though there was no decision that day, the hearing was cancelled. Several weeks passed without a response.

When Duane opened the slim envelope with the City of Akron logo and return address, the one-page letter declared that the vision standard for Akron firefighters had been updated, and he was therefore reinstated to the eligibility list for the Akron Fire Department as a firefighter/medic.

Duane Crabbs was sworn in as an Akron firefighter/medic in the fall of 1992. His internal God-inspired vision for himself was realized through the acceptance of his previously unacceptable physical vision.

Duane's first fire station in Akron was Station 6. He was the new guy again, the low man, but between his experience and attitude, it was an easy fit. Firefighters place a great significance around a firefighter's first fire. Duane's first Akron fire came with the New Year. On December 31, 1992, around the corner from what would, four years later become the Crabbs family home, 975 Marion Place was burning.

The Christmas tree had caught fire. The tree was next to the stairway, which acted as a natural conductor while blocking access to the second floor. The grandmother was in bed on the second floor. She had suffered a recent fall and could not walk. Though there had been repeated attempts to reach her, by the daughter and two men living next door, they could not get past the heat.

By the time Duane and the men from Station 6 arrived on the scene, it was beyond control. There was nothing anyone could do to save the woman on the second floor. EMS treated the two neighbors on the scene. The daughter was taken to the hospital for the burns on her arms and face sustained trying to reach her mother.

The New Year's Eve fatality was a tragic start for a hard year in the neighborhood. That year, Summit Lake would suffer from more house fires—with over $25,000 in damages—than any of the prior twenty years.

It was also a harbinger for Duane's future as a pastor, as he would discover two years later in a neighborhood bar at four in the morning.

~

In the waiting room of Akron General, Lisa and her children waited for news. They were told that Duane had suffered from the classic widow-maker—one hundred percent blockage in the left descending artery, with extensive blockage in three other critical heart vessels. Without treatment, death follows in a few minutes to a few hours. The immediate need was to expand the capacity of Duane's left descending artery. The doctor explained that the insertion of a stent would temporarily improve the circulation.

During the emergency surgery, the family sent out messages to the community for prayers. They waited.

Finally, they were called into a smaller private waiting room. Lisa froze when the woman who came in introduced herself as a social worker. To her, it could only mean one thing. Her husband was dead. He died alone, back in there somewhere. The hospital, the waiting, the private room, and now, the social worker—it was all terribly familiar. She knew these steps. The extinguishing of hope was next, just as it had been thirty-six years ago when the social worker said her father was dead. Her dad, like her husband, suffered a sudden heart attack.

The social worker was talking, but Lisa could not take in the words. Her husband was alert. The surgery had gone well. They could all go see him briefly.

She had run out of feelings. She stood a distance from Duane, her sense of shock turning to something that surprised her—she was angry.

Hannah, Josh, and Jonathan brought Lisa home after they left the hospital. It was as good as it could be. Duane was conscious and himself as he hugged them all. It was the first time in his life he was in a hospital overnight.

Though they were all tired and still wearing the identical shirts, Lisa was full of adrenaline. She came in the house and started throwing out every unhealthy thing she could find. Any snack food, anything past an expiration date, all the other things Duane kept around—his vape and cigars—out. As she whipped through the house, cleaning and tossing, she was looking ahead. She was past hoping Duane would survive; in her mind he was already on his way home. Unless there was a plan, the whole community might consider themselves part of his recovery. It was for her to be the gatekeeper for her husband's survival and reincarnation. She wasn't angry anymore; she was determined. She was ready.

The Arc of Cool

In the 1974–75 school year, Duane was failing ninth grade for the second time. The typical hormonal storm of American male adolescence was accompanied by particular forces that turned the sunny child into a brooding alien passing through the house. Additional fireworks were ignited by his undiagnosed learning challenges, oldest son entitlement, and coming of age in the rubble end of the sixties. All of it together conspired against the stable family environment that surrounded him.

He cut school one day, got high. Bored by the idle afternoon, he went over to Jones Junior High school. He hung around outside, waiting for his friends so he could brag and impress them with his rebel freedom.

As he shuffled home alone afterwards, high on yellow jackets and weed, his mother, a teacher at Grandview Heights High School, was also headed towards the family home in Upper Arlington, a prosperous suburb of Columbus, Ohio. She spotted her son, pulled to the curb, and asked him to get in the car. He was happy for the ride but in no mood for conversation.

"How was school?"

"Okay," Duane mumbled.

This was too much for Julie Crabbs. After teaching others' children all day, she was tired. Her oldest son was at risk. She had grown accustomed to the silence, the sullen posture, the averted gaze, but his lie at that moment crossed a line. She could no longer act like it might change, no longer put a good face on the deep worsening pain in her heart.

She pulled over and stopped the car.

The guidance teacher at Jones Junior High had called her. Duane was truant, again. This would mean another suspension—for the sixth time. He was at risk for failing ninth grade—again. And as he sat there, she knew he was high on something. There was nothing in the slumped figure that suggested her energetic optimistic boy. He had become a stranger to her.

The sight of her disheveled unresponsive son, after a day spent with other parents' sullen children, was more than she could take.

"What are we going to do with you? Why are you destroying your life? You are so smart. You have so much going for you. Why? Why are you doing this?"

Duane hung his head in silence, waiting for it to be over. As her tears joined questions, he wished his mother would just hit him. It would be faster than this. His bad behavior usually evoked silence from his mother. Julie let her husband take on the mystifying changes in the strange boy in the family. With a new manifestation of his delinquency, this was an uncharacteristic burst of anger.

She waited in the silence for her oldest son to respond. This was something new. In the long quiet, her anxious breathing calmed. The gap between them stretched in the heavy pause. When she finally broke the silence, she was utterly calm. There was no anger in her voice. "If you could only see yourself now, how bad you look. Look at me. If I had a camera, you would be shocked. Where is my joyful, fun-loving son? Duane, look at me."

He turned in her direction for a few seconds. It was too painful. He could not handle the feelings arising in him, so he said nothing. He could not look in her eyes because she looked as lost as he felt. He never forgot that moment in the car, because she held the mirror.

"I saw I was breaking her heart."

There came another space of filled silence in the car.

His mother had shifted the terrain of their familiar standoff. Her helpless desperation had been transformed to a language that could reach her son. The tension between the two of them fell away in the silence, leaving space for something new to enter. "What are we going to do with you?"

Her voice had switched to a hard resolve.

"I dunno."

Duane mumbled, barely audible. They were back on the familiar territory of icy distant regard as she started the car.

"Well we can't keep going down this path," she said, as they both stared in silence at the road before them.

His mother's last word in the car was prophetic. That day was the last time he cut school. His last day at Jones Junior High School was an unexcused absence. He would never return.

~

By 1975, Lisa Conti was used to earning her own money. That was normal in her working-class Italian culture of North Hill in Akron. They worked hard. As the oldest girl, she helped her mother on a daily basis. There was a regularity to the traditions of North Hill. Every Thursday, Lisa cut loaf after loaf of bread, filling all the baskets for the weekly dinner at the Italian Center.

However, her job at JCPenney in 1975 was out of the ordinary for a North Hill girl. She was on the Junior Board and Teen Style Council at the anchor store in the Chapel Hill Mall. Such boards were common to major department stores. The members of the council needed to maintain a minimum grade point average and a stylish flair. In addition to acting as promotional agents for store events, the council members modeled seasonal merchandise. Lisa was often featured in the bridal show. Her petite stature, dark hair, and light cream complexion were well suited for bridal, and her personality was remarkably consistent and dependable—she was never late.

Families just like theirs surrounded the Conti family home. Most of the Italian Americans of St. Anthony's Parish arrived in the United States at the same time, in the 1920s, from the same area in Sicily. The community was bound together beyond the shared ethnicity through the traditions of Sunday church and the ceremonies of the social halls. Immigrant grandparents lived in the houses of their children, who came of age in World War II. When the men came back from the war, there was plenty of work out there. The dads worked; the moms stayed home. They steadily paid for their houses and raised their families.

Lisa's father worked at the Ford plant on the west side of Cleveland. Sunday afternoon the whole family had dinner out of her mother's kitchen. In their cohesion around the institutions of North Hill, the Italian septuagenarians and octogenarians were still very active. Everything in Lisa's life revolved around the fullness of the family.

The kitchen table was the heart of the house. Money was often tight. The Contis used the financial plan of a traditional North Hill Italian family. Her parents managed the budget by envelope. They would move cash between the envelopes, trying to keep the debts balanced. There were envelopes for the mortgage, food, the car, church, and clothing. Lisa had the patience to work the envelopes with her parents. She was usually the one to count and roll coins for bologna and bread at Lawson's.

At nineteen, Lisa was participating in the weddings of her cousins and friends. Soon, she would be walking down the aisle with her high school boyfriend, the only serious relationship she had known. There was nothing in her background or circumstance that would give her any doubt about her white picket fence future.

~

After Duane's mother picked him up walking home with his sixth suspension from Jones Junior High School, she and Duane's father Richard talked about what was possible for their son at this point. Julia and Richard were not going to repeat the same pattern of his six earlier suspensions, where Duane was on his own alone. They suspected that watching too much TV was the least offensive of his behaviors on those suspension days.

Their only solace in the ongoing deterioration of their relationship with their eldest child was knowing that they were not alone. Not only had they been witnesses to the countercultural wave in America over the past ten years, but most of their friends were experiencing the same kinds of problems with their once happy children as they moved into adolescence.

Duane and his fellow fifteen-year-olds were the very tip of the tail end of the postwar baby boom. Duane stood a better chance than his wild friends, because he was the oldest in a family with young parents. The friends who were youngest in their families often had far less supervision. Those were the kids with the party houses. Their parents were worn out trying to compete with the influences outside the family home.

Fortunately for Duane, his parents did not stop trying to figure out how to help their son. Fortunate also that Duane had not gotten into serious legal trouble yet. His parents were well respected, they lived in a respectable suburb, he was white, and he was very good at not getting caught.

His escapades covered the range of bad behavior—sex, drugs, stealing, break-ins, property damage, and arson. There were nights he did not come home at all.

Fortunate also that by 1975, there were more choices for youth who could not conform to the conventional path—at least for kids of Duane's demographic. There were alternates to traditional learning environments emerging across the country addressing learning challenges like Duane's. He was a tactile learner, needing contact and motion to take in the world around him. Though he would not be diagnosed until adulthood, Duane had attention deficit disorder.

Richard and Julie did not delay in researching the options, and by the end of that day had narrowed it down to two. Duane was included in the conversation on his future. One option was a disciplined boys' boarding school, an experimental combination of the Outward Bound survival experience and a traditional military school.

The other option was a new program for troubled adolescents through Harding Mental Hospital, only thirty minutes away from home. Duane was not interested in leaving his turf or in anything challenging. He was not sure he needed psychiatric help, but he begged his parents to choose the second alternative.

The three of them drove to Harding the next day. The new facility was behind Harding Hospital in Worthington, Ohio. Nondescript and anonymous, it was a collection of low-rise brick buildings at the back of the property. A line of trees in front and behind the complex gave it a campus feel.

They met with the admitting psychiatrist who listened as Duane's parents talked to each other about what went wrong, blaming themselves, blaming each other, confused. Duane would speak only when directly asked a question, and as briefly as he could.

During the tour, they entered the main youth facility where the approximately fifty resident high-school-aged youth lived. The previous week's humiliation in the car with his mother had sufficiently faded for Duane to return to his now customary state. His still-considerable charm and competitive drive were looking to find the best outcome to enhance his prestige and cool. He pretended not to notice the cute girl checking him out.

Duane, his parents, and an escort walked to a small newer-looking building. The cottage had an easy, open feel, nestled against the trees at the back of the hospital. It was the heart of the program that had attracted Richard and Julie's attention. The counselor also thought it could be appropriate for someone with Duane's behavior and circumstances.

In its infancy at Harding, the Adolescent Day Treatment Program (ADT) allowed those with less severe psychological problems to participate in the hospital therapeutic conditions as commuters. They would come to the program from Monday to Friday, 8–5, but return home for continuity of the rhythms of normal life. The family sat down with the program therapist and a caseworker to discuss the custom details for Duane.

The adults agreed that Duane would be committed to the ADT program. For everyone concerned, it seemed to offer the best possibility for the troubled fifteen-year-old. The hospital staff anticipated a good working relationship with these invested parents. Duane was young, and his behavior problems were a relatively recent development. Duane and his parents were happy that he would be living at home, though for different reasons. Duane could still see his friends; Mom and Dad could keep the family intact. There was hope so soon after the despair of the previous day.

For Richard and Julie, the daily thirty-minute trip to and from the hospital was nothing more than an added part of their daily life. They were taking an action, a step away from the helplessness and fear of seeing the son they loved slipping out of control.

Though he said nothing, and could not have articulated his feelings that day, he remembers it well.

"There was some kind of relief in getting a break. Despite my past behavior, I was reminded of their relentless love. They were not going to let me crash and burn."

The new program at Harding Hospital gave a special status to the small group of commuting juveniles within the resident population. Aside from the capacity to stay in their homes, the five participants in the fledgling Adolescent Day Treatment Program had more privileges, such as field trips.

Duane was representative of this more capable patient profile, and he took advantage of the status to gain position and power. All the patients had school together. Grouped this way, there was a clear tier structure, with the five commuters as the high achievers. This helped Duane, who seemed to be a lackadaisical, indifferent student. Here, he found school was easy. He was no longer in danger of repeating ninth grade for a second time.

Duane found that he could use his charm and smarts to stay within the program while breaking as many rules and honor code pledges as he could get away with. As he did on the outside, he managed to avoid being caught when his impulses took over. On one occasion, he and another patient in the day program slipped away for sex in a stationary boxcar on a siding in the woods.

Aside from his adolescent extracurriculars, there was also the actual daily schedule and routine of the program. Duane listened to the stories of abuse and trauma the other patients experienced. These were things he had never imagined, victimization outside of his experience. Some of the others were taking prescription psychotropic medications. The girl who used sex as a bargaining tool was dosed with Thorazine. She had a vacant stare through half-closed eyelids, a wheezing heavy breath, and a shuffling step. Duane's perspective was shifting. "On the informal ranking among the residents, she was at the bottom. I pitied her. I realized I had made my own problems, had created the situation myself. So I could do something about it, I had the capacity to change. I did not know what that meant, but I knew it was different from some, from most of the others around me. They could not see that in me. I acted like one of them, but I knew that I did not really belong at Harding."

Bill Webb was a social worker on staff at Harding during Duane's tenure. He was not Duane's counselor, so his direct challenge caught Duane off guard. Generally, growing up as the child of a pastor and a teacher, Duane was accustomed to looking interested while tuning out a lecture. He was not prepared, had no defense lined up against Bill's voice. Bill's was a message from an unexpected source, delivered in a manner that aligned with Duane's vulnerability. Bill was blunt and direct in calling out Duane's cavalier attitude: "He mercilessly pulled back the curtains on my cool act, calling me a punk, half-stepping through life, thinking I was getting something over on everyone. He warned me it was only my life that I was screwing up. He made it clear that in a very short time I would be an adult and I, not my parents, would be saddled with the consequences of my foolish decisions. For some reason that straight talk from Bill really woke me up. I knew he was right. The way I was living life was full of shit."

Awakened though he was to the idea of life beyond his current age and situation, Duane did not yet see a way to move forward.

Six months after he first entered the enclave of cottages at the back of Harding Hospital, Duane graduated from both the program and the ninth grade. The prospect of going to Upper Arlington High School in the fall made him nervous. For the first time in his life, he was seeing beyond the satisfactions of the moment. He had always been successful at self-creation by the power of his personality. Now everything was different.

He did not realize that he was starting to process adult thoughts, ideas, decisions, but he clearly recognized things about himself that began to take physical shape. His active explosive mental processes characteristic of his undiagnosed ADHD were being supplanted by the therapeutic daily messages and practices of the previous six months.

He was not confident that he could withstand the pressure of his previous identity. He feared slipping back to the "bad boy."

Fortunately, there was an alternative for Duane. By the time Duane and his parents searched for his next school in the summer of 1976, free schools were a common parallel in over forty conventional high schools. The Linwood Alternative High School was only two years old, but the teaching model was generating tremendous support and interest.

Linworth was the perfect crucible of independent, creative alternate learners like Duane. It was an enlightened educational experiment birthed by a group of Worthington teachers in 1973. The concept of "open class-rooms" and self-determined curriculum had been operating in other parts of the country for over five years.

~

Nearly forty years after he graduated from Linwood Alternative High School, Duane ran up upstairs from his kitchen, returning in seconds with the Linwood yearbook, a well-worn paperbound volume.

He treats the yearbook with great care, placing it down on the kitchen table, opening the slender paperback with a light tremble in his slim fingers. He turns the pages carefully, with a fresh energy and sense of discovery. His excited voice conveyed the fundamental vitality of the experience.

"I was apprehensive about being the new kid—and from a mental hospital, but I found out soon enough that most of the students were new to the concept and to each other. No one was that concerned with where anybody came from. There was too much that was new to rely on old social norms. Everyone at Linwood was pushing boundaries, learning how to negotiate in the radical operating system."

He found the school to be an offbeat kind of place.

"There was a great diversity among the teachers and students. Often it was hard to tell the difference between the two. It was casual. We hung out in overstuffed chairs in the hallways. Each room had a nickname. Art, graffiti, and bright colors lined the walls. There was no authority monitoring behavior. We had sole and full responsibility for ourselves and our own learning."

Duane was an eager student. He thrived in the expansive atmosphere. Independent thinking was honored and encouraged. Students and teachers shared the full responsibility for running the school. It was a living laboratory of community governance.

"Town Hall meetings were my first real experience in the fun and messiness of governance. A moderator was chosen for the meeting and then it started. Each year we had no rules or structure other than what was required by the state of Ohio. All 160 students and seven teachers were present. It was one person, one vote. We decided class schedules. We were responsible for the cleaning of the school-no custodian. We proposed courses of study and determined classroom content and grading. We determined punishments for misbehavior, and we were often harder on ourselves than the school system required. Two unexcused absences was an automatic failure."

The atmosphere of Linwood exposed Duane to ideas beyond the confines of suburban Ohio. He was open to different philosophical ideas, to other philosophies of life. He was still getting high, but not with the destructive habitual pattern of his younger self. He would characterize his use of substances as part of his research.

He recognized that he could make choices through the experience at Harding. At Linwood, he was thriving in an environment of choice. Now his options were not only behavioral, but they were also intellectual, psychological, and spiritual.

He started questioning his native Christianity. He had not chosen this system; he just took it for granted. Exposed to alternate ideas, he thought that indigenous cultures offered a way of being in the world, were a complete system for life. This was different from his sense of modern Christianity. Duane thought of Christianity as a system of beliefs that were mental, that did not operate on the physical plane, were not a design for living.

He started reading books written by or about Frederick S. Perls, the founder of gestalt therapy. "Fritz" had a straight, confrontational style that appealed to Duane. Given his own temperament, the direct engagement seemed to offer real transformation.

He got involved with Young Life in Worthington, partially to avoid the draw into old habits. The Young Life movement gathers school-aged youth, from middle school through college, in programming and activities that are age appropriate while "allowing them to take a good look at the Savior, Jesus Christ."

Duane was attracted to the group because the leaders had great personalities and made it fun. The weekly meetings were held in a different teen member's house, like a rotating club. There could be as many as sixty to seventy teens in the living room. The meetings were held to one hour, during which there would be a stunt or game to establish an upbeat mood. Someone would have a guitar, and everyone would join in singing contemporary Christian songs. A leader not much older than the gathered teens then gave a brief talk about life or Jesus, or both. The meetings closed with prayer.

In 1977, between his junior and senior year of high school, Duane went to a Young Life Camp on Lake Saranac, New York. After a day of topflight recreational sports including parasailing, tubing, skiing, and ziplining, the camp would all gather in the main lodge to hear another message from the guest speaker for that week. Over the six nights, the words were building to the outcome of campers giving themselves to Jesus on the last night.

The speaker for Duane's week was Reid Carpenter. Duane was aloft with the energy and power of the place and the message. So much so that he knew after the second night that he was ready:

"I knew that in committing to Jesus, I was giving up the control of my life as I had known it. It would be that final break between me and the friends and fun of just hanging out. It was the letting go of control, the idea of the leap of faith into... what? I felt God speaking directly into my struggle. My old life was over. God was real. I asked him into my heart at that moment."

~

Lisa's moment of transformation came while she was on a Catholic "Search" retreat at Camp Christopher. With her straightforward pragmatism, she simplifies the most mysterious of events.

"I found Christ, and that made all the difference."

She accepted the gift of faith that had been restored to her without a need to question the validity of its source. This mysterious renewal was not something she could discuss with anyone after she came home from the weekend. No one in her world could talk to her about what happened there. That it happened was enough.

Akron Blues
White Picket Fence

In 1987, four years into their marriage, Duane and Lisa had given birth to a son, Joshua, and a daughter, Bethany. They were looking for a house that suited a family of four as well as the larger family they hoped to become. Important to both of them was being close to their church, The Akron Alliance Fellowship. Otherwise, Duane did not have much concern or yardstick for comparing one house against another. Lisa had the keen eye for the potential suitability of houses available within their budget. And there were plenty to choose from in the West Akron neighborhood around Copley Road, an area composed of neat single-family homes built in the 1920s. The sellers were primarily older white couples, whose grown children moved on as they started their families. The purchasers were like Duane and Lisa, young, middle class first-time home buyers.

1534 Stadelman Street was a solid brick bungalow with a nice yard. It was two miles from their church. There were lots of children on the street, potential playmates for four-year-old Joshua and two-year-old Bethany. Lisa thought the house was perfect.

In the midst of an otherwise sober situation, Duane and Lisa had the capacity to step back and take in irony, appreciate the humor, and then return to the issue with a bit more detachment. It was a habit born early in their relationship, and it served them well throughout their marriage. Once they saw the humor in a serious moment, they both were quick to laugh. It was not lost on them that they consciously chose the house for its proximity to their church, a church they found by accident.

~

Duane and Lisa returned to Akron from their Niagara Falls honeymoon in January 1985. They dedicated Sunday mornings to church shopping. The hunt was suspended on Sunday, January 20, by the coldest day on record in Akron. The temperature all day was between ten and twenty below zero and fell to twenty-four below that night. As their search resumed, they looped around Akron that winter without success. They slogged through the slush of March, discouraged. Nothing seemed right. They wanted a church that was somewhere between Catholic and Evangelical. It seemed like a wide enough net, but not one church they visited left them feeling like they wanted to return

On the last Sunday in March, they saw the sign "Akron Alliance Fellowship" in front of a big Victorian mansion on Diagonal Road. It had a familiar, comfortable look for Duane. He told Lisa it was just like his church, the Fish House, at Ohio State University. The place had been a spiritual home for him, a fraternity of theology and guitars. As he pulled into the crowded parking lot, Duane told Lisa it would be full of Christians like themselves, seeking to make a real difference in the world. He thought the church was affiliated with The University of Akron. Before they walked through the door the first time, they were expecting a young, enthusiastic college church crowd.

They were greeted immediately and escorted to the entry of the sanctuary, the living room of the old house. The room was full, and the usher brought them to the front row, where those already seated smiled and made room for them. Unable to really look at each other, they both felt self-conscious and uncomfortable. There was no choice but to endure the discomfort by behaving as though they intended to be there. As far as they could tell, they were the only white people in the room. It was a Black church.

The heightened awareness of themselves as different, as the minority, sharpened the experience. With barely an arm's length between them and the pastor, they tried to appear relaxed while having no option other than complete attentiveness. "Bloom where you are planted. If you aren't planted somewhere, you will never grow. There is no such thing as the perfect church. If you are trying to find the perfect church, you are wasting your time."

They were welcomed with smiles, warmth, and invitations to return. They did.

It was the first and last time they ever felt uncomfortable in a Black church.

Joining Akron Alliance Church was not a statement, it was a mutual attraction. They were building a home, not a mission. They bought their first house. They were raising a family. The household stayed afloat on the husband's salary. There was the stay-at-home mom. In addition to the modest bungalow, there were two cars in the driveway. They had enough of what they needed, and a prospect of upward mobility accorded their history and expectation.

Though they seemed representative of a typical family in their particular demographic, Duane and Lisa were already outside the curve of their Christian white culture. Operating on one salary was unusual by this time. Despite the efforts of the New Religious Right to reestablish the "traditional family," only seventeen percent of households in the 1980 census were composed of a wage-earning father and a stay-at-home mother. And, at a moment when their fellow white Christian conservatives developed political, cultural, and economic influence by participating in megachurches, they chose to worship in a small African American church in a predominantly Black neighborhood.

Throughout the 1970s, conservative Protestant culture had been gaining strength and sophistication in its messaging. In 1979, Jerry Falwell founded the Moral Majority and became the voice and face of the movement. The movement was primed for a position of influence with the election of President Ronald Reagan in 1980. The Moral Majority stepped with him into the national spotlight as an undeniable political force, a formidable, united, political body.

Ronald Reagan's bootstrap philosophy also included a revolution of economic deregulation. Many stable service professionals found out the hard way they could no longer assume employment security. Duane, a

Cuyahoga Falls firefighter since 1986, had a package of benefits, guaranteed pension, and health coverage for himself and his family. The chances of losing his profession by some external force were small to nonexistent. Firefighting unfortunately would always have a market. It would never become an obsolete job category.

Duane's firefighter schedule of a twenty-four-hour shift "one on, two off" made Lisa a single mom for a full twenty-four-hour day, three times a week. When Lisa was alone with the kids, she navigated the family life with the competence she had learned as a child at her parents' kitchen table. It was second nature for her to connect the family resources with the expenses, meeting the most urgent needs and giving enough to everything else, and still come up with something to "put away." She maintained a balance sheet in her mind, adjusting it like water flowing till it reached temporary equilibrium.

The ease of a conservative family accounting system lifted the worry about finances enough to give joy in the results of her system. The quality of making something out of a lot of nothing was also true of her capacity and quiet competence in emotional situations. The outward calm and attention fronted an internal process of filing the assets and deficits of any set of conditions, be it physical, emotional, or financial.

It was how she grew up and how she was made, and therefore not remarkable to her. The resilience of her character had served her through the grief of the divorce of her brief first marriage. Her faith had been restored and she fully embraced the life and love of the family she and Duane were creating together. In the world beyond the family, she had a sort of trust, a willingness to engage, but she relied on a more cautious instrument, her gut.

The challenge of managing slim resources were minor to her. At the times when they operated with one car, she made riding the bus a special event. It was fun. She and the kids could point at things together out the windows and count all the red cars going by. They enjoyed themselves, talking and learning about the world around them with the other passengers.

She took joy in what for others might be a source of embarrassment. Her children wore clean secondhand clothes. The toys they played with were often pre-owned. Many of the toys had been hers and Duane's. The worn alphabet blocks in their original box were well preserved, solid, and depicted things nearly obsolete in 1990: darning needles, telephones, and typewriters.

It was a white picket fence time for the family. Their lives moved along with a kind of ease that a white middle-class couple could hope for, the best of an intact American dream for a young family of their class, race, and religious beliefs. The only thing that indicated they might be on a different trajectory was their decision to live and worship in a predominantly Black environment.

The family loved the fellowship, the spirit and generosity of Akron Alliance. It was the base of their social and religious life. Aside from the Sunday morning worship together, they grew individually through visiting speakers, Bible study groups, and classes.

Akron Alliance was predominantly a middle-class church, its members in economic circumstances similar to the Crabbs family. Occasionally others with greater challenges came to the church, but Duane noticed that they did not always keep coming back. He and Lisa made a special effort to reach out to Harriet after she came the first time.

Harriet Johnson was a single mother. In an effort to escape her abusive boyfriend and father of her two children, she got on a bus with her children in Atlanta and got off in Akron. Without a plan, resources, or family in Akron, they stayed at the Haven of Rest. Pastor Gus Brown's wife Elaine volunteered at The Haven. As they became stabilized with Akron Alliance housing, Harriet accepted Elaine Brown's invitation to worship at Akron Alliance Church. Duane and Lisa got to know Harriet in the church nursery. Their children were the same age and had become friends.

Harriet lived in Akron Metropolitan Housing Authority (AMHA) housing at the Wilbeth Arlington Homes. Duane and Lisa often drove her family home after church. They were happy to do what they could for her. Finding an extra car seat, diapers, sometimes stopping at the grocery store for her was an easy extension of their own lives.

One Sunday, Harriet hurried over to Duane, excited.

"Duane, Duane, guess what? I've been praying and asking God what I could do to repay you and Miss Lisa for all the kindness you have shown me."

"Aw, Harriet, you don't have to do anything to repay us."

"No, I've been praying on it. The Lord, he told me to take Joshua and Bethany to my house for a night so you and Miss Lisa can go out and spend the whole night together and not worry about your kids. You and Miss Lisa can have a romantic evening to yourselves!"

Duane, unsure of what to say, lied, a typical white lie religious folk use for each other:

"We'll pray about that."

As he went to find Lisa, he knew that this would never happen. Their children had never spent the night anywhere but in their own home. Lisa said nothing and revealed nothing in response to Duane's report of Harriet's offer.

When they did discuss it later, it was not Harriet that was the problem, nor was it the children. They all got along well, and though Harriet was younger than they were, they trusted her, experienced her as a caring and devoted mother. It was where she lived that worried them. She lived in the projects. There could be problems outside of Harriet's control: crime, drugs, promiscuity, violence. How could they willingly subject their children to an environment that could endanger them? It was too much to ask, too much to consider for their innocent children.

They discussed other ways it might work. Could they ask her to bring her children to their house for the night? No. That would reject the gift she offered, her home, and hospitality.

That was the best alternative they came up with, and it was still plain wrong. They kept talking and listening, hoping for something that could cover their worries and Harriet's desire to give back to them.

As they tried to think of a way to spare Harriet's feelings, Duane could not sleep. Despite whatever might happen as a firefighter, his capacity to sleep was rarely interrupted. As he lay awake worrying about exposing his children to potential harm, he realized something. Thousands of Akron's children, God's children, were exposed to these things every night. But he had never lost a night's sleep over the problem; it was only until it became personal that it bothered him.

Trying to manipulate the gift to cover their concerns reflected a lack of trust, not of Harriet, but of God, a god they claimed to trust. This invitation came to them through their own actions in fostering a friendship with

Harriet. They had to come to peace that Joshua and Bethany were in God's protection at all times, whether they were in the projects or their bedrooms at home.

After the successful conclusion of the overnight, Duane and Lisa viscerally absorbed a new understanding of familiar words. The Christian middle-class comfort of "It is better to give than to receive" was turned inside out. Their prior relationship with Harriet, where they had the control to be the givers and Harriet was delegated to be a receiver, was not God's vision. And if it was true that is more blessed to give than to receive, why did white Christian middle-class people reserve the right to the giving side of the equation?

Their relationship with Harriet changed. It was transformed instantly upon the reverse exchange of the commerce of giving between them. Faith had legs; it had muscle. The three of them were peers, their eyes meeting each other in level and mutual, reflected love.

Their experience of the ordinary currency of love was a grounded example of a branch of Christian social action growing within the Evangelical church. Black and white leaders were participating in a renewal of incarnational ministry in cities across America.

"A character is what he does," Cliff Lazar said haltingly, trembling through his message to a small audience at Akron Alliance Church. Duane listened closely, wanting more of that kind of Christianity. Duane showed up that night because he feared no one else would come. Now he hung on every word of the reluctant speaker. The subject that night was John Perkins work in rural Mississippi. Perkins' book, *And Justice for All* had convinced Cliff to overcome a nature so shy that he fainted before he started speaking that night. But as he spoke through his nervous awkward voice, Duane heard the imperative message of the need to build bridges between people of different nationalities and races.

Six months later, Duane and Lisa heard John M. Perkins speak at The House of the Lord, a large flourishing Black Evangelistic church under the leadership of its founder, Bishop Joseph M. Johnson. Dr. Perkins gave his powerful personal testimony of redemption through the power of radical forgiveness.

Perkins was born and raised in Mendenhall, Mississippi. He left for good in 1947, after his World War II veteran brother was shot by police and died on the way to the distant hospital that treated Black people.

In 1960, Perkins felt God's beckoning to come home to Mississippi. He and his wife Vera left the comfort of the life they had made together in Southern California, on the vague urgency of the call.

In the nearly thirty years they had been back in Mississippi, Perkins developed a philosophy of Evangelical Christian practice that asked for more than being born again. Pernicious racism underlined everything, and he saw how it kept both Black and white people in bondage. An activist, holistic approach was necessary for love and forgiveness to replace hatred and fear. He stressed the "three Rs"—Relocation, Redistribution, and Reconciliation.

Duane added John Perkins' books to the stacks that grew around his reading chair. Perkins' ideas came to Duane as he was starting to drift from Akron Alliance Fellowship. He found himself increasingly outside the prevailing views of the congregation. It seemed too comfortable to him, unwilling to consider new ideas as he was experiencing them.

Duane did some of his best thinking and communicating in his car. He was driving a sturdy beige Pontiac at the time. His grandmother handed him the keys when it was no longer safe for her to drive. Though it was old, it was reliable. It only had thirty thousand miles on it and a history free of small sticky children. Vance Brown, his brother comrade in Christian out-of-the-box thinking, could not afford to get his patched-up hooptie fixed. He and his wife Cindy had three girls and lacked the resources of Duane's family support. Vance would lose his job if he could not get to work.

Duane applied logic to the situation. "Kingdom math means freely we have received, freely we should give. Lisa and I have two cars. Vance and Cindy had none. I gave them mine, and we each had one."

Promising to sign it over the next day, he went home glowing from the exhilaration of spontaneous blessing that comes of giving over receiving.

Sharing his joy with Lisa did not engender joy in return. This was not something she could find a way of accommodating. It was not the inconvenience of going back to sharing a car, though she enjoyed controlling the thirty-six square foot area that was her car interior. What really bothered her, what she could not take in one more time was her husband's expectation that she would be happy about such news.

It was his acting alone on a matter of such impact on their family.

She stared at him, her face not moving, not angry, but quite simply set. It was the closest Lisa would ever get to hostility, a face hard for a stranger to interpret, but immediately obvious to those close to her. It telegraphed, "Really?"

It was not the reaction he expected. Wounded, he countered her silence. "It's what God would have us do."

Lisa was calm. She had her own unceremonious logic. "Duane, do you think that it might have helped to consult with me before making a decision like giving our car away? It may be what God wants US to do, but what I don't like is every time God leads you to do something for others, it's at the expense of your family."

Duane still wasn't getting it.

She continued, "You get to be with Vance and Cindy and be all spiritual and experience the good feeling of giving away our car. Then tomorrow when you go to work at the fire department for your twenty-four-hour shift, the kids and I will be stuck at home by ourselves. I won't be able to visit my mom, do shopping, or if anything happens, I'm stuck till you get home the next day."

Duane was on the defense and looking for a solution. He held back from suggesting she could take him to work, recognizing it would mean that the whole family would have to get up earlier in the morning than they would choose to.

"I can take the bus to work," Duane offered.

"Fine."

That simply, without the sympathy he anticipated, his offer was accepted.

Already outliers from the expected middle-class sense of sequence, this taking the bus was to cause deep confusion and misunderstanding for Duane's firefighting brothers. Duane had to board a bus with his full turnout gear, his helmet, and personal equipment as well as a number of books he always brought to a shift. As a junior member of the house, he could never leave his gear at work, because there was always the chance he would be needed at a different house that was short a man. The idea of one of their own reduced to carrying his equipment on a public bus was not just strange or wrong—it was humiliating, shameful to the guys.

Most of the firefighters had second jobs, and many of their wives also worked. They had goals that included bigger houses, better cars, boats, vacation homes. Duane's path was incomprehensible to his colleagues. It was as though he deliberately chose downward mobility. Firehouse humor found his ministry and convictions easy targets, and he took the jibes well. But somehow the bus thing was beyond joking. It made them really uncomfortable.

The consequences of "The Three Rs"—or at least one of the three—"Redistribution"—might be something he needed to remember in advance the next time.

~

On his days off, Duane was a full-on domestic dad. His firefighter schedule gave him a capacity for quick and deep sleep, and an ability to function well despite such erratic slumber. He participated in things with his children that were different than a dad on a more conventional schedule. He engaged happily as a homemaker, in a freewheeling style.

He had no problem disciplining his children, but it was rarely necessary. Their house tended to be the toddler social hub, despite the lack of a universal family standard, a television. As a part-time domestic dad, Duane's natural charm and openness to people made the Crabbs domain safe and desirable. For as long as Josh, Bethany, Hannah, and Jon could remember, that was the situation. They always shared their dad's attention with a lot of people.

Duane and the kids spent lots of time outside on his days off. They went to the Perkins Pool as soon as it opened for the season in June. It was close by, and Duane was happy to take other children who were allowed to go—and could swim. One of only two outdoor pools in Akron, Perkins was crowded, wild, and fun. Josh and Bethany learned to swim there. Often they were the only white people in the pool. Duane was as active as the rest of the crowd, drawing a line of kids waiting for a toss in the air from his strong arms. He encouraged nervous first-time jumpers at poolside into the safety of his catch. They invented games and more games, filling the day to the exhaustion of drying out on the warm concrete deck inside the chain link fence of the chaotic urban oasis.

They were not at the pool on June 16, 1990, the day lifeguard Rocco Yeargin was assaulted, suffering a concussion and skull fracture. Yeargin was pushed into the pool after trying to break up a fight around a lifeguard stand. The situation started with five or six youths taunting the female lifeguard in her chair. It quickly spun out of control. When Yeargin came to her defense, he was knocked into the pool. Attempting to get out, he was kicked back and fell on the pavement, unconscious. He was kicked again, in the head.

Steel plates and fourteen stitches bound his head wounds during his five days at Akron City Hospital. The incident, shocking to some, was not a surprise to others. The park had become a place where activities other than recreational had become commonplace. With the Perkins Recreation Center straddling the 3rd and 4th Ward, responsibility for its maintenance and supervision was compromised.

Black Councilmen Michael Williams and Marco Somerville reacted immediately. With over 150 people in the pool at the time, not a single witness was willing to speak. The pool was drained, the hoops on the back-boards were removed and programming in the rec center suspended. Until the perpetrators came forward, or the community was willing to expose them, the gates would remain locked to all; the neighborhood's greatest summer amenity, including the free lunch program for sixty children, would stay shut down.

The response of the two council representatives was a stand against the 'no-snitch' rule of street law. But the pool incident was a frightening echo of the Central Park Jogger case. The trial of the "Central Park Five" was underway in New York City at the time. Based on what was later revealed to be false confession the five teenagers were sentenced to the maximum sentences their young ages (fourteen to sixteen) permitted for the brutal assault of a loan female runner in Central Park.

Wilding, a term of dubious provenance arising from the media coverage of the case, became synonymous with the image of more than four Black male teens on their feet in the street wearing sweats and caps. The councilmen took a firm, clear stand. They demanded a standard of behavior in a family neighborhood. It was also a stand against behavior that would not be tolerated in more affluent settings. The pool and recreation center were a vital resource in the summer vacation for an entire part of West Akron. The lockdown was a serious blow to the majority of families who counted it as a refuge, a place to see friends, a getaway. It meant that fifty to seventy-five children would go without their daily lunch boxes. Still, the shutdown was a hopeful measure, instituted to reverse a growing destructive recreation inside and outside the public facility. Marco and Mike had to persuade the community that violating the code against snitching was in their best interest.

Duane saw an opportunity for Akron Alliance, an easy natural move from his perspective. The church had recently opened the new wing, a big open space for worship and family programming. Duane and many of the members had participated directly in the construction. Though it had been long and at times divisive, now that it was complete, he and the other volunteer builders felt a sense of ownership and investment in the future of the space. Using it for the lunch program would address at least two issues directly; assuring the continuity of a service for local families and getting the Alliance into the neighborhood they came to every Sunday to worship.

He could sell this one easily. They now had a facility that would work perfectly for the situation. Using the hall was only temporary, until the rec center was back in operation. It was a focused, single purpose mission, helping local innocent families caught short. Other than a few volunteers and the use of the space, it would cost nothing, but garner blessings for everyone involved. He could not think of any objections to the idea as he called for a meeting of the church elders to present the program.

Duane's earlier attempts to bring the Fellowship closer to the neighborhood had not gone as he hoped. He and Vance Brown had a partnership, pushing actions that were less comfortable to the average member. They had similar energy and zeal for doing God's work however it manifested. For a time, they picked up children in the projects to attend church on Sunday evenings. The church was uncomfortable with the behavior of the kids, and asked Duane and Vance to stop bringing them. The church members said that their own children, having to put up with bad behavior at school, needed a place that was serene. Without the purpose of bringing the "bad boys," Ron and Duane stopped coming on Sunday nights.

"Watcha gonna do when they come for you?"[3]

Duane could not forget or leave behind the "bad boys." He had been just like them. He knew the razor's edge between the pose of notorious and the love that does not quit trying to reach the bad boy. Those boys haunted him.

But Duane felt sure that the temporary lunch program would be different. It would be a perfect way to launch the new Life Center building the church had built, a demonstration of their commitment to the community outside their walls. Explaining the situation to the members, he was met with indifference and deflection.

"The building is new. Would the insurance cover any damage?"

"Have we written the guidelines for its use yet?"

"Who would be there to supervise? Who is responsible? What about our stewardship?"

"What about our by-laws? Can we do legally do that?"

Fortunately, the situation at the rec center was resolved, and the pool opened in less than a week. Rocco was back at work the day it reopened, but not all the lifeguards returned to Perkins Pool in June 1990. They felt it was time to leave West Akron.

Duane wasn't leaving West Akron, but he was beginning to feel God's calling to go deeper into the places where others fled if they were able. He countered his disappointment in Akron Alliance Fellowship by looking for new opportunities. He was drawn to places facing the growing menace of trades flowing in and out of urban neighborhoods, with interests contrary to the essential shared idea of neighborhood.

Duane's spiritual turmoil at the time was his alone. The family on Stadelman was stable and thriving. They were surrounded and supported by friends and family. Lisa's major concern at the time was for their oldest, their son Joshua. He was not quite meeting the learning goals for his age. She looked for alternatives from conventional public education to help her son. The home school movement had become a viable and popular alternative, bolstered by the growth and economic power of white Evangelicals. Already a stay-at-home mom, this seemed a potential solution for Joshua's kindergarten frustrations.

Duane's search for solutions outside the conventional led him to a Chicago airport hotel in the fall of 1989. There he found solidarity among a group of 189 other Christian seekers influenced by John Perkins. He drove to the weekend gathering, bringing Vance Brown and Ron Smith along.

The three met people of similar intentions, sharing the passion to find ways of bringing God's grace to the inner city's frustrations. The airport weekend turned out to be the first gathering of the Christian Community Development Organization (CCDA).[+] The exchange of information over the weekend sent the three men with lots of ideas too fresh for pamphlets.

Duane felt he now had guidance for starting an organization. After hearing Alan Doswald from ESA/Love Inc. speak in Chicago, Duane envisioned an Akron chapter. Love Inc. brings area churches together for a united "skills bank" to assist communities of need. Creating such a network was a task that fit perfectly in Duane's personal skills bank. It needed no investment or structure. He could launch it by himself, with nothing but a car, his abundant energy, faith, optimism, and connections in Akron. In his efforts to start Love Inc. in Akron, he went to over 150 churches, all denominations, all over the city. He looked for ways to enlarge his message. He joined the Akron Area Association of American Baptist Churches (AAA-ABC), chairing the Social Concerns Committee. His natural energy, charisma, and commitment to racial reconciliation attracted attention. People listened to him. Love Inc. was incorporated with eight participating churches in 1991. Duane was the volunteer president and Celina Flunoy was the single employee as Executive Program Director. It provided Duane with an institutional legitimacy to expand into the more visionary ideas he hoped to create.

Lisa knew that restlessness was part of the man she married, the man she loved. She did not doubt his love for her, but she hoped that Love Inc. would be the answer to his search. Sometimes she just wanted to ask him, "Why can't you just be content with what you have, with what we have?"

~

Duane's increasing commitments in the faith world did not bring contentment, but only highlighted what he perceived as the split in his life. It was a contradiction he felt internally and recognized as a handicap in building relationships with the African American community. It was a clear disconnect between his work environment and neighborhood life.

Firehouse relationships grow from a variation of battlefield testing; the chasm between sudden danger and stretches of boredom require characteristics that are unnecessary in most urban occupations. It's a too-close and too-long-in-the-house energy, lubricated with taunts and slurs that stay in the house. The discovery of a new perceived weakness in a guy offers a new opportunity for teasing.

In 1990, the Cuyahoga Falls Fire Department was one hundred percent white male culture. The entire Cuyahoga Falls municipal structure was white until the year before, when the first African American employee was hired. Duane could not afford to wait for the fire department to reflect the greater society's complexion and philosophy. He wanted to move in a direction that brought a balance to his whole world view and religious faith. He wanted to work in Akron.

The Akron Fire Department was forced to start hiring African American candidates in June 1973. As would be the case for the inclusion of women in fire and safety forces across the country, the fight for African Americans was the result of a court order. In May 1973, the Akron chapter of the NAACP brought a class action lawsuit against the city, police, and fire departments for discrimination in hiring and promotion. The fifty-one candidates on the eligibility list to become firefighters were white. The 323-man force was white. The NAACP's fundamental contention was that fire and police departments should have representation equal the general population, less than twenty percent of which was Black.

A freeze was imposed, preventing the activation of eight new white trainees until the court determined its ruling. In less than a month from the filing of the suit, Federal Judge Thomas D. Lambros issued his decision, mandating the Fire Department to hire eight Black trainees within thirty days. Time-based mandates were one of the problematic aspects of court-ordered desegregation processes, but time was often the solution to the tension of such decisions as well.

One of the original eight Black trainees, Charles Gladman, steadily rose in the ranks. He was promoted from district chief to deputy chief, in charge of the Fire Training Academy, Emergency Medical Services, and Fire Prevention. He was serving in that position as Duane contemplated applying to Akron Fire. Five years later, on April 11, 1997, Mayor Don Plusquellic appointed Chief Gladman Akron's fifteenth fire chief.

Duane's desire to work with Akron Fire was not an upward or even a lateral career move. It meant a pay cut, increasingly challenging work, starting again as a rookie, and working in a predominantly African American firehouse. By this point in their marriage, Duane had broken the habit of spontaneous solo decision making, and Duane and Lisa were finding ways to work through the differences in their personalities. This new vision presented initially as an obstacle in the steadiness and safety of family routine. Lisa needed time to work through the practical applications of Duane's response to God's call. Such trumpeting trembled the fabric of the known world.

Akron Blues

Patrick Armour

Duane was looking for clues. There had to be organizations and people offering entrance into the places he was praying himself into, other ways of advancing his understanding of the city he sought to "bring God's grace to." He recognized his need for a guide, a mentor, someone already doing the work he wanted to do.

He was not sure what that meant, or looked like, but he knew it didn't look like church. Participation in Community Friends, a Black Quaker church in the Summit Lake neighborhood, was still not close enough. There was a gap between himself and the street of need. As a middle-class white man, he could not close the gap without the right help. He needed a key to enter that world. He didn't know what the key looked like or where to find it but trusted his desire to find God's direction for his passion.

Duane's first exposure to Patrick Armour was through the *Akron Beacon Journal*. The paper ran a series of articles in 1990 about Patrick's effective approach to what seemed intractable crime and drug problems in the Edgewood housing project. Patrick created an organization willing to step in the void. Fathers and Friends was local, Black and male—men committed to promoting safety. It was innovative; it was making a difference.

Duane's second contact was again through the *Beacon*. In 1991, the paper ran a story about Fathers and Friends new center for youth. Duane felt Patrick's personality in his blunt and direct voice in the article.

"Kids want love."

Anxious to move forward in his urban ministry, Duane did not need a third message. He found Patrick's address in the phone book and got in his car.

Patrick Armour was sitting on his front porch steps at 272 Springdale the day Duane drove over. He was spending more time thinking about money. He needed steady income, at least for a year or so, to keep the doors of the youth center open. Patrick saw a real hooptie slowing down, stopping. A white guy, grinning, bounced out of the car, headed his way. Patrick didn't move.

~

Twenty-two years later, through the dark of a Saturday night in November, Patrick was driving home to Tulsa, Oklahoma, after visiting his daughter in New York City. Around three a.m., he called Duane when he realized that he would be passing through Akron in a couple of hours. Duane was already awake and told Patrick to meet him at the café. Patrick had not seen the building yet.

The café was closed, but Duane brought the coffee, rolls, and me to greet his old friend. Patrick was waiting for us in the parking lot. It was still dark and stingingly cold, breath clouding our faces as we introduced ourselves and Duane fumbled for the keys to the side door.

We shook hands. Patrick was sixty-two. His hand could have taken four of mine and still wrapped around to meet itself. It seemed I could have fit three of my selves inside Patrick and still had space to do jumping jacks. Out there in the merciless wind of the empty parking lot, he was like an icebreaker. I wanted to crawl into his wake as we made our way through the gloom to the building.

~

Edgewood Homes was a 173-unit public housing complex, the second oldest in Akron. It was one of three similar projects built in the 1940s to accommodate the massive housing shortage for rubber workers. A series of tidy two-story brick townhouse-type buildings, it was carved out of a neighborhood of single-family houses, a mile and a half from the center of downtown Akron.

The population of Edgewood was one hundred percent white until 1959, the year the Akron Metropolitan Housing Authority (AMHA) moved the first Black family to Edgewood. Akron's total Black population, five percent in 1940, had grown to thirteen percent by 1960.

At Edgewood in 1968, white tenants had shrunk to between five and ten percent. Though the population shift had been swift, Edgewood at the time was a strong healthy community of Black working-class families.

Many of those families had moved to Edgewood after the Grant-Washington neighborhood had been urban-renewaled right out of existence. In that scrubbed landscape renamed as the "Industrial Parkway" there was absolutely no suggestion that anyone had ever hung out laundry or tended a backyard garden.

Patrick Armour grew up in the Grant Washington neighborhood in a stable exemplary family. Though his mother had abandoned the family, his father, Johnny Armour, was a man that everyone looked up to. He had been an outstanding baseball player on several National Negro League teams. He attracted great local attention as pitcher for the Akron Blues. Johnny Armour kept his family of six children together, working at Firestone, where he became the first African American shop steward.

The race riot of July 1968 in Akron played out close to the Edgewood Project. The center of the disturbance was along Wooster Avenue. While not as extreme as what happened in Cleveland a week later, there was tension in growing spontaneous crowds on the night of July 16. Police broke up a fight between groups of Black youth from the north and west sides of Akron. By early Wednesday morning, there were broken windows, rocks thrown, more police, teargas, and arrests. National Guard troops were called, a curfew established. For six days, the pent-up tension and frustration on all sides manifested in confrontations with law enforcement, firebombing of some businesses and hundreds of arrests.[5]

Less than two weeks later, seven people died during an armed confrontation between Cleveland Police and the Black Nationalists of New Libya.

According to several interviews before and after his arrest, leader of the Nationalists, Fred "Ahmed" Evans was looking for a way to back out of the escalating tension without losing face. He wanted out, claiming that he had been in Akron just days earlier when police "had come in and ripped people's hair and beat the shit out of them."[6]

The findings of the Akron Commission on Civil Disorders convened after the disturbances found no evidence of preplanned actions but described the conditions that accounted for the protests. The commission described Akron as a moderate place, without the extremes of other cities convulsed by violence following the death of Martin Luther King, Jr. in April of that same year. Akron had wealth and poverty, but it was balanced around a working population. There was economic stability with low unemployment and responsible leadership, but it lacked daring and imagination.

The same lack of extremes *could* describe race relations in Akron; indifference and apathy, but not extreme hostility or hate. If this only seemed true to the majority white culture, it was in part due to the relatively low, but steadily increasing percentage of Black citizens as compared with Cleveland. In 1970, Akron's Black population was about twenty percent lower than Cleveland.

One side of Edgewood ran along Wooster Avenue, the main site of confrontation. Fear for the safety of the remaining white people living and working in Edgewood led to the Housing Authority's decision to remove all the white tenants and staff during the unrest. After the riot, The Housing Authority's response was to move all the white people—resident families and employees—out of Edgewood.[7]

In the decades that followed, regulations governing Federal Welfare and housing programs gradually changed the population from working families to single women with dependent children. The cost of those policies became obvious in housing projects across the country. Edgewood was no exception. The design of the project itself enhanced the trend to criminal activity. The complex was designed for a different era. The layout of the buildings, with parking on the edges and pedestrian walks within, hampered law enforcement. Cars could not enter the middle of Edgewood, leaving perpetrators unhindered and victims unreachable quickly. There were too many blind spots. Some buildings were taken down to allow cars to drive through, but crime persisted, worsened as new more powerful, cheaper drugs came to Akron.

By 1990, the problems at Edgewood were out of control. Marco Somerville represented the complex as City Council Representative for Ward 3. Almost thirty years later, sitting in the Front Porch Café, his voice and face reflect the pain of a particular memory from those days. "It was a dangerous environment day or night. Lots of drug dealing, shootings. There were two children trapped inside an apartment. Their mothers were dead, killed after witnessing a drug deal. The kids were there, little kids—who got hungry. There were their little bloody handprints on the refrigerator."

Patrick Armour had an idea for Edgewood. Fathers and Friends would operate directly from of the heart of the wound. The problem needed a disaster relief team, moving into the project and establishing a twenty-four hour a day volunteer street ministry.

Patrick took the argument for his organization to the head of AMHA, Paul Messenger. Patrick had a talent for bringing together people who would not otherwise be in the same room. He was a power broker, with the capacity to understand and work with different agents of power in different cultures. He could see through to a vision and could gather the pieces to realize a vision.

The conditions in Edgewood were terrible, but the scale of the problem was not so overwhelming that the parties involved could not interact under the right circumstances if the right leader took a step into it. As an outsider with an outsize presence, Patrick was willing to commit to bringing people together and to creating a presence of care.

He was aware of his capabilities and how to apply them to the desired outcome. With his commanding physical stature, it was as though he could see over everyone's heads to the horizon to the promise of the goal. His particular genius saw the whole array of factors and players in a situation. That vision was expressed in a logic and language challenging to traditional means and methods. It was not at all the expected approach of the board room. In seeing several moves ahead of everyone else, he was willing to shoulder the risks before others could even see the risk.

Paul Messenger saw a partner in Patrick. It was a brave and unusual step for the leader of the Housing Authority to take. It would be a delicate balance between Patrick's citizen-empowered group and traditional law enforcement. But Edgewood needed something fresh and bold. Fathers and Friends was specifically dedicated to making a change in that particular place at that time. Paul and Patrick came to an agreement, and Paul donated the apartment and $3,000 for operating costs.

The custom-made organization focused on changing the conditions at Edgewood through the people living there—and through the people using the collection of low-rise buildings as a drug store. He proposed a different presence of men on the streets: "Men walking the streets, not as policemen, do-gooders or missionaries, but men who understand the problems of the place because they are of the place."

On May 3, 1990, the initiative for Patrick's "twenty-four hour a day" patrol was announced. The group of volunteers would operate out of a Command Center based in the donated apartment at 720 Warner Court. Patrick described their plan at the press conference. "We are not here to drive out the drug dealers. We are here to protect the women and children. Eventually, the drug dealers will leave on their own."

Ernest Thomas, "E. T." was in the first group of Patrick's patrol. Fourteen of his forty-four years were spent in prison. From the minute he joined in, he was all in. He stayed at the Command Center apartment. He understood the predatory world operating at will in Edgewood. E. T. asked his friend Pete Pruitt to join the ranks. Under Patrick's agile leadership and street patter, they did not tell the dealers to stop dealing but to do it elsewhere. If they did not know the dealers personally, they knew their brothers, fathers, a cousin, or an uncle. It was personal. Their presence and techniques started to make a difference that summer. They were recognized, praised, successful.

Fathers and Friends was going beyond its immediate goal of protecting the women and children of Edgewood. It eased out the drug dealers. Patrick and his men were seen as heroes, urban knights of honor. During their tenure in the unit at 720 Warner Court, E. T. found jobs for forty-seven unemployed people, intervened on behalf of eighteen people in legal trouble, and got twenty-three drug or alcohol abusers into treatment.

But the praise and recognition of success brings new problems if experienced for the first time as an adult with a history of the opposite sort. It can be frightening in its unprecedented quality, something never experienced.

It's a stress without a name, and without help navigating that stress, difficult to cope with.

Suddenly, the very thing that the system has been urging you to aspire to throughout a lifetime of trouble, the very thing meant to be the key to a better life, becomes a mystifying threat. No one prepared E. T. for that feeling. How could this thing, success, feel so…bad? No one thought to give someone with E. T.'s background a warning about being congratulated for being *himself*.

Meanwhile, as an independent agency, Fathers and Friends was not covered by AMHA's liability insurance, exposing AMHA to financial loss if they were sued as a result of Fathers and Friends' activities. The board of directors of AMHA terminated the contract in the late afternoon of August 22, 1990.

Ironically, E. T. got into trouble the very night AMHA ended the relationship with Fathers and Friends. He got drunk and aggressive. Stopped in his car by police, a gun was found in his car. He was arrested.

Fathers and Friends moved out of 720 Court a week later. By the end of August, thanks to Reverend Edgar Lee, they took space in Mount Haven Baptist Church at 545 Noble Avenue. Patrick was determined to keep the organization going.

As a result of the changes in Edgewood, the Department of Housing and Urban Development awarded AMHA a $436,300 grant to create alternatives to the drug culture within public housing. The solutions proposed in the application were ideas that were already working thanks to the innovations of Fathers and Friends.

The *Akron Beacon Journal* asked Patrick for his response.

Patrick said, "Paul Messenger and AMHA deserve this grant. They took a chance on us and we knew it. At the same time, I'd like to say that we need people from the grass roots involved. Without that involvement, you've got another canned-soup, bureaucratic program. We can be some help. We need another chance."[8]

~

Patrick and I stand together in total darkness just inside the Front Porch Café building twenty-two years later while Duane goes to find the light switch. It's cold inside but warm enough for the catfish. Water gurgles and drips through the hydroponic system running along the walls of the café, keeping the catfish and a hopeless crop of teeny brave greens alive.

Duane sets up a table with the coffee and sweet rolls, and we sit down in our coats and hats. Duane laughs as he asks Patrick to describe the day they first met. I get the sense that this is a routine they enjoy. Patrick settles down, takes his time.

Speaking deliberately, calmly, he paints the opening scene of their lifelong friendship with a comic's confidence in his delivery. The timing and rhythm have me and Duane laughing before he even starts in. It's the lack of emotion, the deadpan face on the big frame. It's the love of story as a basic value in Black culture:

"I am sitting on my porch steps. Hooptie car pulls up in front of my house. This hopped-up white guy gets out of his car and comes sauntering towards me, big smile. He sticks out his hand, introduces himself, says he had been following me in the paper and he thinks we are going to work together.

"He could be crazy, undercover cop, or I don't know. Comes right up to me with his hand out, grinning."

~

Duane and Patrick talked a long time that day on the steps. Duane knew he needed Patrick and did not hesitate to make it plain. Through Patrick, he could understand the differences between his own world and the world of his calling.

Beyond Duane's one-sided impression of Patrick from the paper was a whole Patrick world of relationships and enterprises. He was a culture broker. Patrick maintained a wide network of friends and associates to make things happen. Duane didn't really fit anywhere into his operating system, but that was also the strength of his operating system, a little bit of every-thing, everywhere.

They sat on the steps together long enough to know enough. Patrick's intuition and style recognized the worth in Duane's passionate sincerity. This white man might be sincere in his desire to really know what it was like out there; this white man was not a conventional kind of Christian. It was a risk for both of them to walk together.

Patrick had relationships with all kinds of different people, businesses, and opportunities. His creativity could weave events together that garnered publicity, accolades, and people. Often the compensation took forms other than money.

Making the monthly note required some agility. The enormous single-story building at 1045 Wooster Avenue was full of activity, but despite the steady increase in visibility, events, and organizations affiliated with the center, the bills still accumulated.

Marco Sommerville remembers Patrick calling about needing a little temporary financial help. Marco's funeral business was young at the time, and he could not spare the cash.

Patrick considered his inventory for trade. "How about chairs? Do you need them? I have 1,500."

Patrick brought the truck to Sommerville Funeral Home in the middle of the night. They were nice chairs. Marco gave Patrick three dollars a chair. He still has some of those chairs twenty years later.

~

We are sitting at one of the smaller round tables in the café. Though I'm taking notes, I have to remind myself to do so, because it's hard to take my eyes off Patrick as he speaks. He speaks a poetry, mixing past, present, and future in a floating association of big and small concepts, thoughts, memories, and feelings. It's unique, familiar, and utterly strange.

He mixes me into it all as the architect of the building we are sitting in and as the writer he sees me becoming. His words make the pen in my left hand vibrate. Duane's tape recorder picks up what my notes would never capture; the brilliant cadence of Patrick's mind tracing a partnership of mutuality.

"Why are we doing this? It's a natural question.... It opens minds and hearts. Of the intelligent and the most wounded. I am here to help. That is the architectural piece of it. You are here to take that language of construction and develop it into a verbal/visual process of the everyday walk and hands-on ministry and all.

"At the time, Duane was struggling to become an Akron firefighter paramedic by day and by night he wants to be out with the brothers.

"Duane introduced me to his mom and dad, brought Wanda and me into his home life. Rich, his father, was a kind, quiet man, told me about what he had done in Akron, Cleveland. Impressive. During civil rights time, a major force for good and change. Then it made sense on the how and why of Duane. His parents became mentors for me and Wanda. Rich asked me to mentor Duane, to watch out for him...."

Patrick paused, tears in his eyes.

Duane, quietly, "They were a little worried about me."

Patrick chokes up, not just a throat-clearing thing. He has to stop.

After a minute they both laugh, switching to another memory, a time Duane was excited about a building, and brought Patrick to see it.

Patrick turns to me with the deadpan stare. I laugh with Duane in the pause he takes before speaking.

"Trees. There were trees growing through the roof. It had some connection to Firestone. I thought it was a bad idea. We were doing ministry, I wanted to tear down the ministry, and find the connections. History, so much more than 'let's do some ministry.'"

I wanted to ask what Patrick thought of Duane having a building now. Instead of trees growing through the roof, there were catfish swimming around us in murky waters of coffin-sized Plexiglas boxes. As the architect, there were times I wanted to tear down the building and start from scratch.

～

Patrick introduced Duane to bar life first through the VFW Post within walking distance of Duane and Lisa's house. Bringing his new sidekick through the tavern door with him was a necessary part of their time together. Bars and clubs were essential meeting places for Patrick's operational style.

From the neighborhood bar, they started to go to other spots on Patrick's map. Late one afternoon in the beginning of their relationship, Patrick and Duane parked next to a nondescript building in South Akron. It was a social club, and that afternoon was to be Duane's baptism in serious barstool ministry. Aside from a brief period of typical college bar drinking as an Ohio State freshman, Duane had no experience or understanding of bar culture, though he knew what it was to get messed up. In his early teen years, Duane was the ringleader who could charm adults to buy alcohol. The woods of his Upper Arlington neighborhood were his bar.

Patrick rang a buzzer, and the bouncer greeted Patrick warmly. Patrick's stature was so big, the guy didn't notice Duane at first, but stopped him with a look when he did.

"It's okay, he's with me," said Patrick.

They walked towards the bar as Duane's eyes adjusted to the darkness of the club. Of the dozen or so patrons in the place, Duane's awkwardness was heightened. He was the only white person. As Duane pulled up a stool, one of the guys shooting pool called Patrick over.

"Grab a seat, Duane. I will be with you in a minute."

Whatever cover he might have had coming in with Patrick evaporated when Duane sat alone at the bar. Though he wanted to be a pastor of souls, he looked like a cop. His cool firefighter self was starting to sweat. This discomfort was not part of the evangelical crusade he anticipated. He ran hot to Patrick's cool. He tried to keep his coiled energy neutral, to keep the gaze of his wild sloping eyes level.

He aimed for the nonchalance of a regular customer when the bartender asked what he wanted. He paid for a beer. He left the change on the counter. The beer gave him something to hang on to. A few seats from him, a young brother started talking to him. He turned his controlled steady gaze towards the young man, listening. The young brother was telling Duane in very graphic terms about his sexual exploits over the past few nights.

Duane could hear Patrick's voice somewhere behind him as he kept his focus on his drinking companion at the bar. The monologue was steadily unfolding into a story about beating up a white guy. Duane did not react. He just looked and listened to a sprawl of smoking wreckage. Panic fluttered at the edges of his eyes. He sensed this might be some test of will, and he felt violated and trapped. His beer was getting low, and he told himself he would not order a second.

This was outside his realm. He wanted out. Patrick's voice and laughter seemed a mockery of his distress. Duane felt a pressing aloneness in this room of men.

He also determined that if it was a test, he would endure. There was nothing he could say in response to the man's enjoyment of Duane's discomfort, so Duane just tried to seem cool.

When the brother left his spot to use the bathroom, Duane rose in an act of manufactured ease and wandered over to the pool table. Patrick was at ease, his attention on his friends as they talked and played. He seemed oblivious to Duane's attempts to catch his eye. After a long minute, Duane managed to get Patrick's attention. Patrick shifted, offering Duane just enough distance from the action for Duane to come alongside.

Cue stick loose in his hands, without breaking the casual mood, Patrick smiled at Duane. "What's up?"

"I'm uncomfortable," Duane hissed.

"Good." Patrick replied, quiet and slow, barely audible.

"No, I said. "I'm really uncomfortable."

"I heard you and I said good."

"No." Duane was trying to get his point across. "No, it's like, time-to-leave uncomfortable."

"Duane, if you walk out of this bar right now, everyone in the place will be able to smell the fear on you."

"But—"

"Lean into it," Patrick rumbled, and turning from Duane to his friends at the table.

Duane thought of walking out but did not want to be seen as fearful. He sat back down, now more angry than afraid. The young man came back, and Duane just sat and listened, too full of complex emotions to do otherwise. After a few minutes, his companion moved on to another conversation. Duane was grateful for his barstool as the adrenaline drained away. He swirled the remaining beer in his glass, relieved of the tension of calculating every move. He let go. This was not all about him. There were worse things than discomfort. Lean into it.

The barman nodded to Duane's empty glass. He met the eyes of the barkeep, considering a second beer. As still as he was now, a simple gesture was enough to indicate no thanks.

After about ten minutes, Patrick came up and slapped his huge hand on Duane's shoulder and smiled. "You did good."

Angry, Duane wanted to know if it had been some kind of hazing.

"Well, let me ask you a question first. Why do you think people come here?"

"To get drunk," Duane said as he tried in some way to urge the mountain of Patrick towards the door.

"Wrong. If they want to get drunk the same amount of alcohol is half the price at the corner store. They are not paying double just to get drunk. Okay so why are they here? Look around. CO NEC TION. You see that bartender? He hears more sins confessed in any one night than a priest does in a month. Except he ain't offering them wine for absolution. He's giving them something to help them cope with their pain, but it won't take away their sins. Could be before the night's over they commit a few more. And you felt uncomfortable walking in this place? How do you think they feel walking into your church? So no, this is not a hazing. It's just an exposure. If you really want to be a good shepherd, you are going to have to give up the home court advantage and get more comfortable with the lost sheep."

For Patrick, his physical stature was intrinsically part of his power. He knew it, and he used it. He rarely needed to do anything more than stand firm to achieve dominance. Duane felt the strength of Patrick emanating from the stillness in his body. There would be absolutely nothing to move him until he was ready. Patrick's experience, pain, brilliance, and leadership were in the world because he knew what his skin on his massive frame could do, because his eyes were higher and could see more and farther than anyone else in his world.

So when he even leaned down to his friend Duane the next moment, it was an enfolding, a gesture of humility, and a profound signal to the room that this crazy hopped up honky was *someone*. He slowly inclined his head to Duane's ear. "Look around. Connection. They come for nourishment, for fellowship. Why do you think I brought you here? These are the people. If you're uncomfortable, lean into it."

Patrick touched his shoulder. They walked out the door, sun still shining, two men.

~

The sweet rolls lay on the table, unopened. Duane made a second pot of coffee. It was cold in the café, but doing anything other than sitting together at the round table was not a consideration. It was the only place to be, it was the center of a pool of illumination.

Patrick did not vary his cadence as he carried the through line of moments and impressions. "It's what you do with your personhood. Imparting humanity. The reality of 'no matter who you are or what you are, you are important to the world.'

"South Street is Duane and Lisa. Because that is what it was before they got here, because it was about people, because it was a gathering place in this community. They moved to it. When others moving up and out, they moved in. Quit the day job. Moved to it. Left the hero job. Middlebury has their story. Do they have a Duane and Lisa? Go back to the beginning…go back to the beginning. The story is what it is.

"In America, we want everything to be instant, a stick-on or punch the key.

"But my impression of Duane is that what makes him different not only as a guy, a white guy, minister, part of all that, not young but not old, part of that—part of many things…the makeup of him, what makes him unique. I recognized it then, over twenty years ago. In these times, his essence and operational style—which makes him, as some folks would say, always late but always on time—is conflicting because that is the challenge in our relationships—to be so familiar with something but also to not know why it is so familiar…maintain the alive spirit—and the enigma—always new, full of contradictions. The spirit of South Street Ministries, the program, the ministries, the personality of the place is who he is, who Duane and Lisa are. It is not fake; it is not a program that is developed out of some think tank or some great idea. It comes out of people who are committed. It is verbal and non-verbal.

"And that conversation is very different from what we are hearing from the political or religious arena, how the church sees the mission of the church. How is it that the Vatican—for as long as they have been doing what they have been doing—and how is it that this new Pope Francis—who is basically doing what Duane has been doing—can seem so weird? But so right. Why is that?

"I had guys change on me. Duane never did. Never did. He stayed. Made that choice. Trust them, Duane and Lisa, anywhere, with anybody. People only as good as their own personal interests."

~

There was no curriculum for the internship with Patrick. Duane was the only student working the streets with Patrick for a while, but they were rarely alone. From those late-night walks in South Akron, Patrick revealed the law of the street. Duane could accommodate the uncomfortable. It never was or would be his world, but it was a world he wanted to understand, that he knew he needed to know and be known by.

This was the incarnation of his calling to serve the urban poor. There was no other way and no turning back from slowly walking with Patrick down the middle of Long Street at two a.m., preventing the car behind them from turning onto Princeton. There was no way but the way of stillness, sitting on the top of the steps of the Lincoln School at three a.m., not moving as a silent figure carrying a long wooden staff approached him steadily, stopping in front of him, staring hard, then turning away. This was the way into his ministry for a new suffering. With Patrick, he learned the language. His body absorbed the law—lessons fortified him for the day-to-day and night-to-night reality of the lives of the urban poor around him. In the months that Patrick stayed in their living room, this was their way of apprenticeship.

This was the upturning of the logic of firefighting. This was fires burning everywhere, and there was little he could do but watch. Or at times not watch, at times turn his head and detach. By his presence, there was complicity. By his presence, there would be suspicion. But with Patrick, he had the pass.

Perhaps he trusted Patrick too much, but it was not a debate he could afford to explore at the time. Duane knew Patrick had enemies and a reputation for crazy. He was grandiose. In his job as a debt collector, he would rise up on his toes, magnifying his already impressive stature to make it clear that a storeowner best have the outstanding debt due when he came back.

Despite his size and measured pace, he could be fast. One night late, the two were walking home down East South Street. Patrick had just successfully diffused a tense encounter at an all-night gas station at the corner of Grant and South. A swarm of police cars descended on the BP Station expecting drug dealers who had scattered away and found Patrick and Duane instead. Under the taut glare of adrenaline and station lights, Patrick's move was to reduce his threat level in his own way, not theirs. He brought down the tension by turning himself into a clown, harmless, a court jester in the spotlight.

Relieved and unguarded afterward, as they passed between the county jail and the strip club, they were surprised by a young brother who came alongside in a manner that Patrick took as disrespect. He whipped his arm around, taking the young man's jaw in the grip of a bulky ring, pulling on the side of his mouth. Patrick seemed to enjoy the obvious pain his hold of forced submission was causing. Duane felt the pain of it as he watched, his mentor becoming something else before his eyes. Patrick released the young man after making his point about not sneaking up on a brother. The guy ran off, the pride wound greater than the physical. Duane's pain was a layered thing, the sudden overturning of the reverent table, the separation of dark and light gone, all to gray.

Duane did not have a place in himself for this side of Patrick.

Where it had seemed until that moment that Duane had no choice but to trust Patrick in any situation, now he had a choice to make. Patrick crossed a line. Patrick showed his wounds, and when the hero does that, it feels like a betrayal. Patrick became a man. Patrick had flaws.

Duane Crabbs responded with a grace that would often be denied him as he deepened his faith walk in the coming years. He stayed with this Patrick, the whole of this Patrick. There would be more unexpected sides of Patrick, when his demons gave rise to paranoia, but Duane did not take the exit door.

He ran to the pain as a firefighter. He was struck by how something as unpredictable as the work as a first responder in emergencies could now seem so logical and traditional in comparison to the nocturnal work with Patrick. In all of his years with Patrick as his most important teacher, Duane never saw any fear in Patrick. Duane in his act of faith, brought with him the instincts of the firefighter; a pounding heart running with active compassion, taking up the suffering of another culture, one with its own logic.

When Duane walked alone, he learned to turn his head at the right time as exchanges were made. He had nothing but his clothes and his prayers on him. No money, no need for whatever was being sold. He carried the contradiction of running with Akron street and returning home to his sleeping family. As a firefighter he had seen suffering, but that pain was within a system he knew that allowed him to be an agent of protection and immediacy, to relieve the pain of the suffering. This was a much deeper and vague suffering.

Though they never returned to that first Social Club, Duane's tutelage in bar ministry was ongoing. Along South Main Street in the 1990s, though most of the commercial life was gone, there were still thirty nightclubs, bars, taverns, grilles, and strip clubs. Ted's Bar, today the Catholic Worker's Peter Maurin Center, was one place that continued to draw a steady crowd. Operating since 1962, owner Ted Bahry could recall a time when you could get anything you wanted on South Main Street. In his early eighties, he still lived above the bar and made sure that everyone felt welcome at Ted's. Competing bar league ball teams went to Ted's after games. It was the friendly place, the bar that Patrick and Duane could both just be easy, be themselves.

Patrick had a friend in mind for Duane, Claudia Palmer, the owner/manager of another bar a few blocks down the street, the Main Event. Like Patrick, she oversaw a raft of enterprises. She was born smart and poor, one of four children, growing up in two rooms with her parents in the barrack housing on the east shore flats of Summit Lake. The temporary Quonset colony had drifted into permanence after the wartime rubber workers moved on. She grew up navigating the system through the combination of her fierce intelligence, adaptability, and the power of West Virginia hills running in her blood. Claudia started working in South Main street bars when there were three shifts at Firestone. At fourteen she was a prep cook in the morning, getting breakfast set up for workers coming off third shift.

When Patrick brought him to the corner of West Crosier and South Main Street, Duane was not particularly impressed. That part of South Main Street had fallen on hard times. Two old brick buildings shared a party wall and a parking lot. The first was a strip club. Patrick and Duane passed by that and walked into the other. Claudia Palmer was tending bar. To Duane, walking in the first time, it was nothing more than a dive.

~

The sun was well up by then, and it was time for us to think about getting up from the table. This was a familiar routine for the two old friends. Patrick and Wanda had moved to Tulsa after Wanda became the Oklahoma State Director of Rhythmic Gymnastics in 1994. Patrick never really felt at home in Tulsa. He would return for this and that project that he and Duane engineered, often staying with the Crabbs family for months on end as they worked on a project.

Patrick tilted his head down for a moment and came back to a point he made before. "I have had guys change on me. Duane never did. Never did. He stayed. Made that choice. Trust them, Duane and Lisa, anywhere, with anybody.

"Do what you do with your personhood. Imparting humanity. The reality of "no matter who you are or what you are, you are important to the world. That is leadership agility. Chew gum and walk. It is what he does. People who spend all the time in the spiritual world do not know how to do that. They end up doing a lot of stuff that is a cover up. Leadership agility—on the football field, like ballet. Leadership—Mother Theresa out there, doing, while the other nuns are behind the wall. Agility."

After launching a successful small conference designed to bring area churches together, Duane and Patrick ramped it up the second year, renting the Knight Convention Center. "Seek the Welfare of the City" was a reflection of the energy, originality, and aspiration of the partnership. On a Friday evening in Fall, the Knight stage was filled with key local church members, over one hundred singers, and headline speakers John Perkins and a former Klan leader.

But the crowd on stage looked onto an audience of 700 filled chairs and 2,300 empty chairs. Though it was the first citywide event that had ever happened with that degree of breadth and unity, the free event did not attract a crowd. Their confidence in the idea obscured the need for vigorous promotion, particularly since it was scheduled in direct competition with local high school football.

Patrick stayed with Duane and Lisa during the strike by Local 684 of the AFSCME union, when the striking hospital workers took to the picket line two weeks before Thanksgiving in 1996. They were protesting Summa's intention to diminish the union's numbers by hiring non-union cleaners.

Local 684 was sixty percent African American, ninety percent women. Many of these women lived in Summit Lake and similar neighborhoods. Working between the key union leaders, both of whom were white men, and the hospital administrators, Patrick and Duane were another conduit for conversation during the bitter negotiations and equally bitter weather as Thanksgiving passed into Christmas.

They operated outside the common channels. Duane, ready to jump to resolution, would feel Patrick's big hand on his shoulder.

"Relax, Duane. We are still on divine time."

In the twenty years since the Armours left Akron, Patrick and Duane had maintained a working friendship. Looking back on those times, Lisa would say she was relieved when Patrick would go back home to Tulsa. "I was not involved in what they were doing together. I knew it was edgy. He was such a big presence. But there were no red flags with Patrick. I had a high level of trust. My kids loved him."

~

Our tour of the building was very short. Patrick seemed tired, and it was past time for him to get on the road. The two men, bonded as brothers after twenty-two years of freelance street ministry, would visit on the phone for hours until the next time they saw each other.

It was a long way from their first meeting on Patrick's front porch to a cold morning farewell at the Front Porch Cafe. Another goodbye was just part of their rhythm.

Though enduring and deep, their partnership was afflicted with blind spots. The shared manic optimism about what they could accomplish together obscured the obstacles in their path. Their unconventional intelligence and energy did not fit the conventions of a system, so they found a different way to run together, a kind of spectacular three-legged race.

It was the last time they ever saw each other. Patrick died seven months later in Tulsa.

Duane's sense of loss was devastating; Patrick, his confidant, friend, and brother, Patrick, his mentor and the closest he had ever come to a partner, was gone.

The Coast of Tyre

In June of 1991, Lisa was pregnant. The whole pregnancy was difficult, and by the start of the third trimester, her doctor ordered complete bedrest. Duane's mother took care of Joshua and Bethany on the days Duane was working. When their father was home, it was an entirely different household for the kids. Dinner with Dad was a big shift from Lisa's organized, focused singularity in the kitchen. It was more of a game, all hands on, Duane wrapping the kids in oversized aprons and putting them on stepstools to help him. It was a cross between firehouse chow time and camping culinary adventure. Duane, Joshua, and Bethany managed to use a lot of dishes to make a batch of instant au gratin potatoes, which Josh dismissed as "egg rotten" potatoes. The fun of the time helped offset the strange food and the even stranger fact that their mother was present but not there.

During the time Lisa was on bedrest, Duane continued to take the children to Community Friends Church on Lake Street in Summit Lake. One Sunday, a small boy came into church alone. Duane invited the unusual guest to sit with him and his two children. The eight-year-old white boy, Scotty, could see the church through the windows of his house directly across the street, and he just crossed the street and came in. Scotty lived closer to the church than anyone inside the sanctuary, including the pastor.

This was the typical condition of urban churches by the latter part of the twentieth century, whether they were Black or white. The size of the parking lots grew as the congregation dispersed to the suburbs, returning only on Sundays. There was an acknowledgment of this unfortunate condition, but it had happened gradually to the point where there was no denying it—churches were cut off from the neighborhoods that surrounded them, properties that the community moved around, not into. Community Friends was mostly Black, mostly middle class. The appearance of Scotty that Sunday had import beyond the occasional local who was drawn in by the coffee and doughnuts over the Good News.

Duane was a natural magnet for children. Duane immediately got on eye level of any child. Though the sudden appearance of his adult elfin gleeful face might have been startling, within seconds all resistance would melt. He had the magic to bypass all stops and go straight for that part of a child most essential. A two-minute encounter with Duane could provide the care and love that trailed years into the future. The physical grace and strength of a working man was balanced by the compassion of his soul and the trained instincts of his profession. There was nothing that kept him from the immediacy of a child. His radar could sense the timorous beating heart of the child disappearing behind a grandmother's legs. Within four minutes, lifted airborne by Duane's upstretched arms, they were weightless and laughing.

Rather than go to the back of the church with the Crabbs kids and other children during the service, Scotty snuggled next to Duane and fall asleep under his arm. Duane and his children walked him home and met his mother, Brenda. As Scotty became a regular, Duane found out a bit more about his home life. There were plenty of men who came to the house, but after they were in the back bedroom for a while with his mom, they were gone again. Duane could never convince Scotty to join the other children—he just wanted to stay with Duane.

Despite the difficult pregnancy, Hannah was a perfect healthy baby. After months of confinement, Lisa was happy to be back in the world to show off the newborn girl to the gushing enthusiasm of the whole congregation the first Sunday she was back at church. Scotty sat on the other side of Duane and elbowed him, pulled to whisper in his ear.

"Who's that, Mr. Crabbs? Is that your old lady?" he asked.

Duane chuckled.

"I don't think she would appreciate that, Scotty, but yes, Lisa is my wife."

"What's a wife?"

Duane laughed again, thinking that Scotty might be teasing out of some jealousy. "C'mon Scotty."

"What's a wife?" Scotty was seriously asking the question. Neither the word nor the concept was in his experience. Men and women came and went from the house he and his mother stayed in. It was the restless moving tribe of the addicted who, like his mother, were seldom without the need to find the next draw of relief on the pipe.

On the way home, Lisa listened to her husband spinning his thoughts. "How is a kid like Scotty going to make it? I mean, how are any of these kids going to make it?"

She had no idea or answer. She was simply happy just to be back in the world, in the car with their newborn, looking at the scenery outside the windows.

It was normal for Duane to work things out behind the wheel. He mused and thrashed that morning that the couple of hours a week in church would barely touch the surface of need. How he was struck by the difference between the message in the gospel inside that church and the reality of the crack cocaine across the street, and the impossibility of bringing the two together the way he was doing it. If they were to live the calling to follow Jesus, it meant living it every day.

He felt it immediately—it was the next stage of the mutual contract, their incarnate journey with the poor. It meant they had to live in the neighborhood they claimed to care about.

"That's it! We are supposed to move into this neighborhood! It's what God wants!" Duane, swept up in his idea for their next step, was surprised by Lisa's silence. He looked over to see the trail of tears down his wife's face. His elation vanished as he realized he had again overwhelmed Lisa with the inconvenient extravagance of his unprovoked ambition for others over the needs of his family. It was not a new problem, merely the replay of their pattern at a particularly vulnerable moment for Lisa. His idea for tampering his impulsive brainstorm was to ask Lisa if she would at least pray about moving into the neighborhood.

Silent no more, her emotions burst in a bawling response.

"Yeah, I'll pray—I'll pray we never move into this damn neighborhood."

Already outliers from expected middle-class ambitions in all their circles as well as their families' sense of sequence, the very consideration of such a thing would enhance the loneliness of their choices. Duane and Lisa did not "fit in"—not within their work environments, not in their home school group, and not within the church. Their faith in the call of living out their faith sustained them as a couple against the prevailing questioning and subtle humiliation from each of these sources. As each decision brought them deeper into an incarnation of their faith, they still found a way to remain in, if always marginalized.

In the three years after Duane's Summit Lake Epiphany, the subject of moving did not move. Duane's excitement about the idea only strengthened Lisa's resistance. She kept her defenses solid, all too aware of his charming, compelling, persuasive will. The idea did not advance one inch since the day it burst forth.

Fortunately for their marriage, it was an issue over there, and in front of them was the fullness of family life. If they kept their conversations to the matters of the day, all was well. They were busy years. Lisa was home-schooling; Duane was working and continually seeking greater connection to ministry. They had their fourth child, Jonathan.

They continued to worship in Summit Lake. Lisa knew that often after a shift, Duane would drive to the neighborhood at night alone or with Patrick. Working, going to church there was fine with Lisa, but living there? No. She did not change her answer whenever Duane brought it up. Eventually, worn down by the persistence of it all, she decided, as a wife, that she could follow her husband's vision and said she agreed. She was resigned to it.

But it was Duane's turn to say no. He told Lisa it would not happen unless and until she owned it. This was unexpected. It always felt so pushy. That is what she was used to through the three years of Duane's vision. Suddenly it was something else. He gave her the power.

"Until you feel one hundred percent that it is right, it is not happening."

With that, he stopped talking about it. He did not bring it up again. This new ground allowed her to relax, to pray with a new an unguarded openness. The wall she built around her heart to the idea fell away. She could release the idea of the white picket fence. It was a fantasy, that idea, just somebody else's sense of what life should be for her and her family.

Lisa's description of her unusual decision is brief and direct.

"I just knew, like I was freed from something that had been a weight to me. My heart said yes, this is right for us at this time. This is what Jesus is calling us to do as a family."

~

It was the day after Christmas, 1995.

The house was not on the market. The house was not even visible from the street, despite the leafless trees. From where they stood at the foot of the driveway, they could see the rooftop if they swiveled their heads a bit. Duane and Lisa had seen the house from the outside earlier on a tip from Miss Julie, one of the mothers in their home school group. Its command of the landscape was obscured by the angle of the hill and the tall weed trees of neglect. Fresh inches of snow softened the harshness of the impossibly steep unpaved driveway. On either side of the driveway, the forest of scrawny urban ailanthus trees rose, forming a kind of archway that could seem almost welcoming.

Duane and Lisa stood with their four children on the sidewalk looking up, waiting for the arrival of friends and Gloria, Miss Julie's mother, who in her mysterious ways had secured the key. There was no address at the driveway apron. The overgrown driveway was easy to miss, and there was nothing indicating the address, but the family of six standing together on West South Street, not at a bus stop, just upright in the cold, was impossible not to notice.

Joshua, their oldest child, loved the place instantly; it smacked of adventure. The steep driveway, perilous to an adult driver, was magic to him. It was a sledding hill to Josh. Above the uphill passage, Duane and Lisa knew that the obscuring dense trees yielded to a space of light—and the house broke free, a solid presence commanding a broad view framed by an establishing line of Interstate 76-77 in the foreground and downtown Akron floating above the freeway's constant low hum.

The house was condemned. The windows were boarded up with notices posted from the health department. Unbeknownst to them, it was scheduled for demolition.

From the outside view, Lisa thought the generous foursquare had potential beyond its current scars and hardships. It was big, for one thing. They were a family of six now. Dave Baker, one of the two friends along for the tour, stepped to the back door with his crowbar to pry off the plywood.

They had only been looking for a home for a few months, but it had been nearly four years since Duane had introduced the idea of moving to Summit Lake. Over that time, Duane often cruised the streets of South Akron after his twenty-four-hour shift at the firehouse, seeing a life of greater purpose possible by living there.

The first Summit Lake house they had toured was something Duane thought could be perfect—it was a fortress. The home of convicted drug dealer James Dillehay, it had lots of security and special features. However, it also shared a driveway with the house next door, where James Dillehay's cousin lived.

The house was cleaned out by the police, its contents hauled off to join other confiscated bounty from drug busts in the nineties. In what was the original Firestone factory on Sweitzer Avenue, Dillehay's belongings joined the cars, boats, and the more conventional array of firearms and scads of ammunition. Because houses could not be hauled off to storage, two plain-clothes detectives accompanied Duane and Lisa through the property. Dillehay's cousin watched the tour from the other side of the property line. The house boasted an elaborate camera security system, no windows less than eight feet above the ground and reinforced steel entry doors. The second floor featured a big Jacuzzi tub in the middle of the spacious master bedroom.

However, Lisa's list of house minimums included bedrooms for the children. Creating the impressive master suite came at the cost of losing all the other bedrooms. Beyond all other considerations, this obvious impracticality eliminated the house before there was need to ponder the potential advantages—or the potential wrath of the neighbor. To Duane's relief, as they left the property, Lisa was oblivious to the hard stares from the other side of the driveway. Duane acknowledged the flat unbroken mean mugging in their direction, grateful the plainclothes officers assured a quick exit without incident.

There was no lack of available properties in this part of town in the nineties. However, two-thirds of the houses were now rental property. The population of the Summit Lake neighborhood had been declining since the 1960s, but in the 1980s, the pace quickened in a steady downfall as the economic power and city resources drained towards away, and drugs trafficking flowed in.

The few other houses they had seen since the fortress all had at least one big major no. The backyard was too small, the houses were too close together, or the basement was a pond. Her discerning eye was not an indication of resistance to the neighborhood itself. Over the years of participating in the church life and ministry in South Akron and praying for the understanding and participation in her husband's vision to move to the inner city, she was sincere in the search. It was simply that the houses thus far did not meet the needs she saw for her family. Lisa was—by nature and upbringing—practical and traditional. The reality that they were forging new traditions in their marriage did not phase or alter her approach to decisions. Once she was convinced of an action, she brought an unjaundiced common-sense view to counter Duane's buoyant immediacy.

By the time they toured the inside of the house with their children and two foundational supporters of their ministry, Dave Baker and Paul Tell, Lisa knew they had found their home. The sense of its potential from the outside view was reinforced by the interior plan, the arrangement, and flow of the rooms. Her consistent priority was whether the house met the needs of her family, with a second consideration of its potential for their unfolding ministry. The house had so much to offer in both categories. There was a big backyard. The garage included an apartment above it. There were four big bedrooms upstairs and an airy attic for a fifth bedroom, playroom, or office. There was the potential for each child to eventually have a room of their own. The downstairs, with work, could be a generous open flowing space, plenty of room for homeschooling and the outreach to the neighborhood Duane and Lisa envisioned.

Baby Jonathan and four-year-old Hannah stayed in the arms of adults that day. Josh and Bethany made a game of picking their own bedrooms on the second floor, gleefully blind to the clutter and debris. Their joyful claims of ownership shaped the expression of a unique family on their uncharted journey.

Reinforced by the assurances of their friends of its structural merits and their commitment to pursue the title and renovation, Duane and Lisa came to the decision in mutual excitement. Lisa's vision saw the potential of the bricks and mortar of their future. Duane's vision was the potential of souls to be saved through the container of the house. They found a home base for the journey inward, a commitment to follow the message of Jesus Christ through their mutual commitment to live as they were called by faith.

Before the group left the house, they stood together in the remains of the kitchen. It was the moment to pray into the hopes and fears of living out God's calling to "seek the welfare of the city."

It was the day after Christmas, 1995.

The Price

By Christmas 2005, the family had been living in the house on the hill for nine years. There was a stretchy rhythm to the Crabbs family life that expanded the immediate family to those staying on the living room couch and front porch day bed. Jon, the baby, was twelve. He loved the guests; his easy nature embraced them as playmates.

Patrick Armour, Michael Starks, and Derek Foster were uncles. Derek especially was his buddy, staying with the family for months at a time over the years. As special hangout buddies, the unlikely pals watched television together when the rest of the house was sleeping. With no vocabulary for strangers, his natural grace was a speedway to friendship. In the time it takes to shake a hand, his arm was over the shoulder with a big smile that, like his father, transformed his wide dark eyes into arched lines.

Restrictions that applied to his three older siblings loosened up by the time Jon was careening around the neighborhood on his bicycle. He was allowed to go to the houses of his neighborhood friends. The corner store was still off limits, but now and then, his bike would be in the heap outside the rugged old building just up the street from his house, a quick stop catering to quick needs. While the kids scraped and pooled their money for candy, the adults of the neighborhood did the same for loosies, lottery tickets, and single malts.

The neighborhood was porous. Kids snaked through blocks, easily cutting through backyards, up and down, their dirt bikes swerving and braking, kicking up waves of loose earth. They made trails and pathways that suited whatever new idea they invented. There were all kinds of outdoor games, always stuff to do and always lots of kids to do the stuff with. The Crabbs yard was open on all sides, a nexus of crossings, an elevated fort, a citadel, the home base of games, the place that kids screamed out "safe" as they touched the swing set.

In the tumble and hustle of temporary alliances in a gang of kids, Carl and Jon were always on the same side, special friends. They were almost exactly the same age. Their houses faced each other, separated only by the property line between their two backyards.

For as much as they were brothers, there was a stark contrast in their home lives. Carl didn't know his father. At his house, his mother Roslyn's boyfriend threatened and terrified his mother, him, and his younger sister.

When Roslyn made the decision to leave her boyfriend, it meant leaving the house they all shared on Bachtel immediately, with her two children. The Battered Women's Shelter had space for her, but there was a problem. Carl was thirteen, and the shelter did not take boys older than twelve. Roslyn called Duane and Lisa. They assured her that her son would be safe and welcome in their home for as long as she needed to take care of herself and her daughter.

What had been Friday overnights for the boys became every night. Their typical boy domain had two single beds, two dressers, and a closet. It was Jon and Carl's room. School was the only time the boys were apart. Carl got on the bus in the morning for Innes Middle School, and Jon walked into the living room, his classroom of two-and-a-half students. Bethany, as a high school senior, was the half student. By this point, she was in charge of her own studies as a post-secondary student at The University of Akron, anticipating college. Hannah was in the eighth grade and wanted to be the first of the four children to go to regular high school. The following fall, she would enter the freshman class at Archbishop Hoban High School.

The weeks became months. Thanksgiving passed, and the house took on the shimmer of Christmas. There was no restraint on the celebration of Christmas in the Crabbs family. It was a special time, just the immediate family, in pajamas and robes, making the most of the morning. Though it was timed out in the rhythm of opening presents, the deeper beat was the rare intimacy of just them, just the six of them being together in the living room without the prospect of anyone coming by. There was nothing but being together, each in their usual spot, all cherishing the precious singular excess of it all.

The house on South Street was the only home Jonathan had ever known. He was two years old on the day after Christmas, 1995, when the family saw the house for the first time. It had taken a full year to renovate the house, and this was the eighth time the family was in the midst of the biggest celebration of the year. The birthday of Christ burst open, a kaleidoscope of joy in the Crabbs family.

For Jon, the house was the center of his whole world. It was his school and his playground. It was the platform for endless games and exploration. Waking up on Christmas morning, the best present Jonathan could ever imagine was waking up too, across Jon and Carl's bedroom.

There was a rhythm to the household that extended the family to a lot of other people. Jon loved the full house. But this morning was different. Carl was his friend and his brother. Jon was about to open a whole new world to Carl. The presents were a part of that, but more than that it was a unique time for his family. What made it special was its protected status; time for just the immediate family in an enactment of ritual that grew annually in the quality of its preciousness. Now Jon had the chance to open this exclusive door to Carl, to show him what Christmas could feel like.

Amid the raucous joy of breakfast, Jon leaned to Carl and whispered, "Welcome to the family, brother."

Carl had seen his mother and sister a few times after they moved into the Battered Women's shelter. The contrast with his situation at the Crabbs house was stark, but never more so than Christmas, and he could not find words to go with the emotions. Looking at his pile of wrapped gifts, it was his turn to whisper to Jonathan. "I just wish my mom and sister could be here with me."

Carl had to keep asking about the pile of gifts. He could not believe they were all for him.

The family liked taking a long time to open gifts, one by one with lots of teasing and comments about each present. As they started in, there was a knock on the door. Duane jumped up, thinking it was most likely a stranger, since all who knew the family understood that Christmas morning was not the time to stop by.

Carl's mother and sister were standing outside. Duane was shocked. Months had passed without a word from Roslyn. He stepped outside and closed the door behind him, stung by the contrast of the warmth outside and the cold immediacy of the unexpected Christmas guests.

Roslyn wanted her son to come with them. Duane weighed her maternal rights against the interests of the young man inside as he glanced to the car running in the driveway, seeing the boyfriend she had tried to leave behind. Asking them to wait in the car, he turned back inside the house.

Duane called to Lisa over the joyful noise in the living room. They discussed what to do quietly before Duane stepped out, containing his emotions while striding over to the passenger side of the car, his bare arms cranking a sign to lower the window. He thrust his head into the car with a simple short message. "Unless you come back with the police in a police cruiser, Carl will be staying here."

The kids continued in the fun, oblivious to the flash encounter. Their shaken parents whispered in the kitchen, deciding, hoping, that this would be the end of the story for now, that the episode was over. Duane and Lisa slipped back in the room as they had left just a few minutes earlier, their reentry as unremarkable as their absence. The unfettered joy of the kids made it easier for Duane and Lisa to put aside the sting of what had just happened by ignoring what had just happened.

Roslyn returned in a cruiser a half-hour later.

This time there was no option. Carl left with a few clothes and the one gift he had opened, a basketball.

Duane had to explain to Jonathan, "We have no choice but to let him go. It's his mother's legal right to take her child."

This was not the first time, nor would it be the last, that a child who felt like family had that status revoked, but the immediacy of Carl's departure on Christmas seemed particularly cruel, impossible to understand or accept. The family wept with Jonathan.

Though words seemed slight comfort against an onslaught of such devastation, it was all Duane could offer in the void. Jonathan remembers his father's words because they were impossible to accept. "Everything happens for a reason." What possible reason could there be for what happened?

Everyone wanted to believe that Carl would be back soon. For months after, all the things he left on Christmas stayed in Jon's room. The unopened presents were stacked in the closet.

Jon could not reconcile what had happened. Duane and Lisa had created a family and faith life that was neat, safe, where everything fit, and God was benevolent. Suddenly none of that made any difference at all.

This was the thing that Duane and Lisa could not protect their children from. The consequence of love freely given came at the risk of incomprehensible heartbreak.

This was the price they paid for love. It was not that their kids were hurt by the perceived dangerous neighborhood, it was the price of love that they learned about at an early age. It was not the troubles of the neighborhood that cost them, it was the love. Love in a place where things are often temporary, and the idea of control is just that—an idea. The reality of not counting on anything lasting—but love anyway.

Carl did sneak back to the Crabbs one time, against his mother's orders, but Jonathan was not home. Duane and Lisa didn't tell Jon. In 2014, Carl called Jon. His mother eventually left her boyfriend for good. The family moved to Virginia and everyone was doing okay.

The two friends stay in touch by phone.

Light Glass Block

There it was—Light. Predawn, distorted, and cold, shining through glass block, it was still a good sign to Eric as he pulled into the parking lot of the Front Porch Café. It meant Larvett was inside, setting up the kitchen for breakfast customers. Eric had another new idea for attracting more business for the café and hoped Larvett was in a mood to hear it.

The new idea had just occurred to him while he was sitting in his car, in line at the café's competitor, McDonald's. More fortress than golden arch, this Mickey D's was between the café and the access ramps to the expressway. The place netted all the suburban commuters looking for a quick bite before work. Further adding to his irritation, this McDonald's was drive-thru only. The walking poor—most of the neighborhood—were shut off from service.

Parking at the far end of the Front Porch Café lot, he crumpled up the paper from the sausage and biscuit, stuffed it into the pocket of his hoodie, and grabbed one of the eight coffee mugs he forgot to bring into the house last night, again. As he crossed the parking lot in the Akron winter gloom, he heard distorted contemporary gospel music blasting straight through the walls of the café, another good sign. Larvett Carlton only played music when he was in a good mood. Eric pulled out the giant ring of keys as he approached the steel front doors. He knew pounding on the door was useless with the praise music at full volume. "Larvett, turn down the music, man, I gotta talk to you."

Eric's official job at South Street Ministries was building construction manager, but there was no limit to what landed on his table. All five staff overlapped in the evolving space of the ministry. The Front Porch Café was their field of operations, welcoming in the surrounding neighborhood.

Eric had no prior construction experience. Characteristic of Duane Crabbs' enigmatic "hunch and a prayer" leadership, Duane trusted Eric with getting the donated building into habitable shape. Eric was the guy to take the "church without walls" into whatever it would become now that it had walls.

"The first miracle in the Front Porch Café was that it did not collapse while I was trying to save it," Eric loved to say, typically punctuating the joke with his distinct laugh, something between a loud cackle and a guffaw. He had no vanity about sharing his ineptitude in the construction trades, how his incompetence was continually upstaged and saved by God.

There was a wide margin for mistakes at South Street. Duane was fond of saying that the ministry was "faulty but not false." His messages about the walk of faith being a collaboration with God was reckless to many, but Duane and Lisa led by example and made the unconventional seem normal. Lisa and Duane were a conventional middle-class American Christian couple, but the life they were creating was outside the curve of their demographic. They chose a path of poverty that did not include a recognizable safety net. The building gave them a larger platform for the expression of a faith walk, and that faith permeated everything. Of the five employees, only two—Lisa as the administrator and Larvett as the chef—had any claim to work experience in the jobs they held.

Twenty-nine years old, Eric was a big solid guy, with a bit of extra plush under his perpetual hoodie and jeans. The kind of guy one would choose to hide behind if a threat came forward. His bright red hair was thinning on the top, but awesome on his chin, a shiny copper beard framing the smile that revealed perfect straight white teeth. He was quick with his signature duck call of a laugh, and it was loudest and most frequent at his own expense. In the early days, he was one of the burly trio of benevolent bouncers for those stepping beyond the tolerance threshold of behavior inside the café. It was a pretty high bar in a situation without any real rules. How can there be rules in a place that declared itself a domain of "unlikely partners taking shared risks." The loose flavor of the day-to-day operations was formed from the leadership and charisma of Duane Crabbs. It was born of his sauntering walk of unconventional, enchanted trust, his firefighter emergency respond-er personality. Masculine energy bounced around the café, oblivious to the incongruous insistent gesture of Lisa's touch—a vase of seasonally appropri-ate plastic flowers on every table.

Eric smoothed out the McDonald's wrapper on a plastic checkered tablecloth and called out again. "Larvett! The music! I got an idea."

Larvett, in no rush, turned down the music as Eric waved the McDon-ald's wrapper at him. "You went to McDonald's? I'm not talking to you."

"No, man, listen—we make a healthy breakfast wrap, have our own drive-thru, better and cheaper than them!"

Larvett drew himself up, head lifted, mouth puckered, wearing the face of chef-street smart imperial inscrutability, another good sign from this mercurial man. Larvett was interested to the point that he dropped the opportunity to give Eric a hard time for going to McDonald's. Eric let it go for now.

Eric had been working for South Street Ministries for three years.

Still in its infancy, the café was cultural mash-up; some Evangelical storefront worship on Sunday, fundamental Akron AA recovery space during the week, and a diner that still felt like a beer joint. Overlaid on that mix was an ambitious murky new age quality, thanks to the constant gurgle and drip of a decidedly garage-style hydroponic system along the perimeter of the dining space. The happenstance of all of that stamped it M.E.N. at work. Carol Murphy, a self-described atheist who called Duane Crabbs her pastor, referred to the place as "Jesus' frat house."

Eric Harmon arrived in the typical fashion for South Street, a ramble, tumble, and fall into grace. Serving in the Ohio National Guard's 135th Military Police Company in 2003, he was among the first wave of American military entering Baghdad after the collapse of the Iraqi forces. Though two members of his unit died in a mortar attack, he does not blame anyone but himself for his later troubles. He never romanticized or exaggerated what happened there and had little tolerance for those who did. "Most of the time, we weren't doing much more than hanging around."

He came back to Akron in January 2004, but it would take much longer to find his way home. He had grown up in a family who identified themselves as Christian but did not go to church. His parents' divorce was long and difficult for him and his siblings. His grandmother was a devout believer. If only for her sake, Eric's mother took her three children to Akron Baptist Temple for the church youth group. After Eric came back to the United States, that connection to faith and any sense of purpose in life were gone. He was putting on a show, going through the motions of finishing a college degree while his real homework was gambling, drinking, drugs, and women. He got away with lying and lies and lied some more. He lied through his beautiful smiling white teeth.

Close to finishing his degree, he left The University of Akron, signing up for Officer's Candidate School. He hoped things might change for him at Fort Sill, Oklahoma, but all his new vices came with him and grew. He was a messed up, big guy, and he made a big messed up situation. He spent all his money and more that he didn't have, married an exotic dancer on a whim, and robbed a gas station to buy her a ring.

He was in no hurry as he drove away. When the police stopped him less than a mile from the crime scene, he said nothing and offered no resistance. The evidence was in the passenger seat. He had not bothered to move the stolen cash, his mask, or the hunting knife he laid on the counter when he asked the young woman at the register for the money. He was cuffed out in Oklahoma, twelve hundred miles from home on April 5, 2007. It was his twenty-fifth birthday.

After pleading guilty to robbery with a weapons charge, a second-degree felony in Oklahoma, he was sentenced to two years in Lawton Correctional Center. On his way to prison, Eric realized he had felt nothing for so long, he did not recognize at first what he was feeling. He was afraid. Unable to block the fear, he cried for the first time.

Recognizing that no one got him there, he did not expect any favors from anyone. Eric knew enough to know his thinking was messed up. Solitary confinement reduced him to time and space with nothing but a life of the mind. Without anything to sustain a future, he tried to think of a time when things were different, to recollect a happy moment. Memories of his time with the Akron Baptist Youth Group came to him. It was a place he remembered as free—and maybe that was what happiness looked like. He kept having flashes of memory of that time. With nothing but his aloneness, he waited for something more, maybe guidance, instruction from the memories as they became available to him. He began to think of his child-hood exposure to Christian behavior as training for his present condition.

It was the beginning of something new for Eric. Unencumbered with responsibilities, he moved with the desire for something different to fill the time. Struggling with letting go of doing things his way, he paid attention to the messages from AA meetings, seeing himself not as an alcoholic, but definitely an addict—to lying. He took things a day at a time. He got better, he felt better. As his release date was coming, with still eight months to serve, he was afraid that he was having just a jailhouse conversion. "So one day, I had this idea. Why not give God *all* of me, I mean one hundred percent of me for just one full day, just for today?"

One day turned to a string of days.

He stayed straight and used the tools available during his time inside. After a while, reading his Bible and learning how to exist in prison, he felt something more than the memory of happy. He was happy.

He saw his incarceration for the gift that it was, something that demand-ed that he stop. He felt freer than he ever had. The lying was done, over, gone. This now, this moment, this ground, this concrete, this here felt so new, so promising. He had a chance to start over.

He laughed at the irony of incarcerated freedom.

Eric was granted an unsolicited early release date. His sentence was reduced to fourteen months. But this prospect only added to his unex-pected growing fear around getting out of prison, a ballooning dread far larger than the fear he experienced coming into prison.

He had a way of seeing that looked around the next corner, and the view was catastrophic. He knew the statistics on recidivism—high, over seventy percent—just as he knew about the weakness of jailhouse conver-sions once out in the world. His Bible-based connection to Jesus could vanish on first temptation. In the weeks before he got out of Lawton, he fasted, prayed, and worried.

His grandmother in Ohio was also worrying about his release. Outside of family, she had no one to talk to about her troubled grandson. Her church was very conservative, and she feared the judgment and corrosive gossip if people found out that Eric had committed armed robbery.

The one friend she confided in invited her to a prayer service. Duane Crabbs was the pastor that night. After his introduction included a mention of his weekly Bible study at the county jail, she could not wait to talk to him. He would understand that her grandson was not evil. After the service, she quietly managed to tell him about Eric. He said a prayer with her aloud on the spot. She never forgot the gift of understanding he so freely and lovingly gave her, without a shred of hesitation or judgment.

After fourteen months in prison, Eric returned to Akron. Within the first week, he went to the Wednesday night worship service at his childhood church, Akron Baptist Temple. He saw a lot of people he remembered. Hank Richards, a tall, lanky, older gentlemen with the fire-and-brimstone type of Evangelical Christianity particular to Akron Baptist Temple, invited him to his Kingdom Builders brunch on Saturday. His old friend Matt Simpson offered to pick him up for church on Sunday.

He was surprised on Sunday when Matt pulled into the same parking lot he had been in the day before. In Akron less than one week, he was back inside the old shambled brick building a second time. The atmosphere inside seemed more like a party than church, but everyone looked happy to be there. He tried to stick with Matt, to blend into the background as much as his stature would allow.

He thought the pastor, a balding energetic man named Duane. He seemed kind of crazy, but "he had the whiff of Jesus on him."

He thought this was a church that might work for him. It was as raw as he felt.

When Matt offered him a place in the house he shared with two other guys in South Akron, Eric accepted without hesitation. Within his first week in Akron, a place he could worship and a place to live had found him.

He carried four years' probation and the employment stigma of a felony. There were few options available to him for work. He was hired by a collections agency and spent the day on the phone chasing debt, then driving to collect. It was okay for a while, and he was effective and resourceful with many of the calls. He did not have any problem collecting on those who he felt could pay up. With others, with people who he sensed were honest but burdened by poverty, bad luck, or bad decisions, he some had discrepancy to forgive debt. But never enough for all the cases he wanted to. After a few months, the phone meant nothing but dread to him. On the repeat calls, he would develop feelings for the clients. There was one Mexican family he had gotten too close to for his line of work and had been delaying making the last call. His boss said he had to close the case by the end of the day. He wanted to get out of his job, the weight of it all was too much, but so recently out of prison, there was nothing else out there.

Feeling desperate, frightened in a new way, knowing he needed help but was unable to figure it out how to get it, Eric wanted to go see Duane on his lunch break. He resisted, not wanting Duane to feel any pressure to act on his behalf. He quit anyway, and started volunteering at First Glance, a youth organization in Kenmore. Duane found out about Eric's situation and called him. "Eric, can you tell me how much you would need to live for one month?"

Such a practical question was not what Eric expected, and came as a kind of whack in the head of his terrible thoughts. Before the robbery, his rank and experience gave him a large salary. He made and spent a lot of money. As fast as it came in was as fast as it went out.

Now, here was Duane offering a creative and immediate solution, and he really had no idea about how much he really needed.

"Maybe like $750?"

Duane offered to hire Eric for one month and take it from there.

At that point, even a month of an extra small paycheck was a stretch for South Street. But Lisa managed to put it together. This arrangement continued for a second and third month. When Duane asked Eric to think about how much he would need for a year, he gave it more time. He was starting to believe he could really make a new life in Akron.

"$26,000."

This was not an amount the shoestring ministry could afford. Only Lisa and Joe Tucker received paychecks, as part-time administrators. Duane did not draw any salary from the ministry. Duane had a natural confidence in high wire crossings. That confidence was bolstered by the simultaneous paradox of continuous feet-on-ground life he and Lisa made together in Summit Lake. Without any clear idea of how this could be done, he and Eric prayed over it, and wished each other a Merry Christmas.

Duane got a phone call Christmas Eve from a government official, asking him to come to the courthouse. This was someone Duane had gotten to know in escorting people through the court system. The official wanted to remain anonymous and explained that it had been a good year. A great admirer of Duane's work, the official was giving him a contribution, and his signature was required. As a government employee, a document was necessary stating that the donation was freely given, that there no reciprocity of favor as a result of such exchange of charitable personal donation.

Whenever Duane was given money, his custom was to accept with gratitude, regardless of what was offered. He simply put any check into a pocket without looking at the amount. Later, he and Lisa would look at it together. Lisa opened it as they stood in the kitchen of their home. The check was for $25,000. They could give Eric a job for a full year. Four years later, the renovation of the building was far from complete, but the lights were on in the café, and Eric was getting paid and paying back.

~

The staff and volunteers did everything in the café space. In its prior life, it was a Croatian American banquet hall and still clearly bore the hallmarks of the genre. Seen from the outside, the plain brick building on a street once filled with similar workaday structures did not indicate the surprise of the interior. The features of the banquet hall were immediate and intact beyond the solid metal door—a stage, fluted metal columns up the center of an otherwise open space, and a pressed tin ceiling. The inviting warmth of the space was the signature feature by necessity and purpose. The necessity part was the lack of suitability of the rest of the building, and the design part was the reflection of Duane and Lisa's partnership, a combination of confessional and kitchen table.

But tucked throughout the building, there were the hideaways. In the back room, a one-story addition to the original structure, hodgepodge piles of donations grew over what had been a barroom and banquet service kitchen. Small paths ran through the jumble of secondhand equipment, bicycles, and clothing, opening onto small clearings with two or three chairs. They served as impromptu counseling campsites, handmade confessional booths hacked out of the donation wilderness. For some reason even he could not explain, retired hospital Chaplain Lin Barnett loved counseling in those urban caves.

The second floor was divided into fourteen small chambers. In its last legal use, the upstairs had been a men's rooming house. All the copper plumbing was long gone, but it was otherwise intact. It had a spook house feel to it, accentuated by the skinny tall corridor running straight down the center of the building. The finish on all the plaster walls, doors, and windows curled in licks of dried oil paint. Much of the plaster ceiling was on the plank wooden floor, crunching under the pressure of foot traffic. When the ministry took over the building, it became the not-so-legal residence for Freddie Jones. Among his other odd jobs, he was night security. Freddie loved it up there. He wired up some temporary lighting. Nobody bothered him, and for the most part he followed the one rule: no cigarettes or alcohol inside the building.

Going in the basement was not for the nervous. The stairway was dark and draped with cobwebs and exuded a musty dampness. Just looking down was enough to discourage most tourists. Down there was the ultimate masculine refuge. Chef Larvett, his assistant Thomas, Joe Heindel the carpenter, Freddie, and Eric had carved out lounge space. The ceiling was too low for any legal human occupancy, but the low height supported low-slung slouching. The circle of discarded lumpy couches around a coffee table received a speck of natural illumination from the meager light coming through the dirty frosted wired glass of a window well facing the parking lot. The only décor was a ceramic toilet and the odd empty snack bag or Arizona iced tea bottle. Joe Heindel rigged up a semi-private shower for Freddie. The basement was otherwise filled with objects of unknown provenance plus the belongings of temporarily homeless friends, accented by crates of mysterious industrial spindles. It had the feel of a deliberately staged firetrap.

All the men working at South Street had the love of Jesus in common. And, other than Duane and the two Joes, all the men had incarceration in common. And other than Duane, all the men had bachelorhood in common. The basement was their lair of freedom, an impromptu clubhouse refuge from the unpredictable traffic of the café, the perfect break room, a frat house for Jesus. Eric, by massive key ring and by natural touch, was the undeclared leader of the cohort. If Duane was not around, Eric was the next guy to solve a problem.

Eric's first and ultimately successful building challenge in the fall of 2010 was a total roof replacement. The original flat, commercial-style roof was rotten. A donor provided the funding to replace it. In what would be the wettest September in memory, Eric sweated his way through the installation. He stayed several nights with Freddie on the second floor, under the stars and exposed ribs of the new hip-style roof. The two men managed to keep most of the water out with big plastic sheets covering the openings.

That summer before the new roof, the café had a parking lot kitchen, with Freddie manning two grills. The complete exposure of the operation made for some unique street theater on Grant Street. The customer base already supported the work of the ministry, so the sight of Freddie flailing about the kettle barbeques as friends arrived in the parking lot was a preview of the South Street experience.

After the launch of the inside café, Eric was looking forward to having more time for the ministry part of the job. He was no more suited to this work than he had been to managing construction. But everything about South Street was a walk of faith, right down to the bacon and eggs.

In the first month after his return to Akron, Eric kept his connections to the church he knew from childhood, Akron Baptist Temple. He was willing to do anything to keep his faith strong. He participated on a few night missions. It was a practice common to evangelical urban ministry. Talking Jesus in gay bars and strip clubs didn't make sense to him, but he had been willing to try, to be part of the team. But not only did it not work, he felt like a fraud, acting friendly to someone who interpreted his beautiful smile as something else entirely.

But mission work was completely different at the café. Opportunities kept walking freely through the front door. Duane's idea was for a place that landed between the bar stool and the church pew. He wanted a neutral space, a third space that was not at all about proselytizing. He described a place of true equity, of deep listening, of conversations across the barriers.

Eric's efforts to cultivate deeper friendships had not gone too well. Eric could be patient. He tried to apply his love of fishing to his work. He could stand in a stream and cast a line for hours, not particularly concerned about catching a fish or not. He thought about how he could pray as he ambled around in the woods, looking for edible mushrooms, but totally content if he came up empty. But as his efforts seemed to go nowhere with the Akron street congregation, his desire to land someone in the Jesus column grew.

Eric's work in linking jobs for people wanting work was slow, but at least, so far, one hundred percent successful. Of the four people he placed in jobs the previous year, all were still working. For those new hires, reliable transportation was a perpetual challenge. Entry-level jobs in manufacturing and assembly were far from the old urban neighborhoods where his placements lived. Keeping the guys employed often meant Eric was the chauffer. It sometimes meant he made the 5:30 wakeup call on the way to pick someone up. He stayed easy with it, even if it meant three wakeup calls on the way and waiting in the driveway. "That's my job," he would say. "That's what Jesus would do."

The day-to-day work of the building never stopped. Between the maintenance demands of an old building, there was the emotional triage coming in off the street. The café was a new entry in the mash-up of social and religious outcroppings in the neighborhood. The locals were testing out more than the menu of the place, they were sampling the staff as well. Most of Eric's early part-time hires ripped off the café or just stopped coming in for work. Interest in the spiritual offerings of the café tended to flame high and die fast.

The walking-distance patrons were testing its limits, tolerance, and manipulative potential. When the café first opened to the public, it was impossible to get any sense of what was inside. Glass block and brick filled in what had been large storefront glazing, and the single leaf front door was solid metal with a dent-dappled finish. Walk-in traffic expressed needs way beyond coffee and eggs, and the café did its best to meet each person where they stood.

Duane led by example, engaging each person coming in with equal dignity, real questions, and conversation. He made a quick study between the genuine and the hustle. The slope and clarity of his almond eyes concentrated the intensity of even the most casual of his gazes. With energy boiling out of him most of the time, he could still come to a flat stop and receive. The man could listen. It was authentic when his listening led him to ask the person if he could say a prayer.

Eric and the other guys watched Duane dive into all kinds of broken. They saw him also with the less obvious broken, those in business suits. Out of earshot, they would watch as Duane's comforting hand reached slowly to meet the subtle drop in the shoulder as the person felt safe enough to just let go of the facade.

With a tremendous energy driving his dedication, Duane's first responder experience and personality took his tremendous energy directly to the person or place of greatest need. He had a capacity for seeing through the defenses and the heart to protect the subsequent exposed vulnerability.

Eric and the guys saw and experienced the equally powerful fury of his indignation, righteous or otherwise. If someone was gaming him, taking him for a fool, Duane could flare. With lightning-strike speed, Duane was instantly in the face of the offender, nose-to-nose, finger jabbing the guy, an intense, fierce reproach tightly hammering against the shocked face of the offender, body leaning away from Duane's frontal attack. Quickly ignited, quickly quenched, unforgettable to the subject and the witnesses.

The triage atmosphere, scarcity of resources, and youth of his male apostolic staff created a kind of duct tape solution to building and personal problems. It manifested in countless ways and made for a kind of freefall creativity sensitive to the next crisis. The church without walls was figuring out how to live inside the walls.

In the heady atmosphere of crisis management, a solution that is "good enough" often becomes permanent. The first indoor kitchen operated inside an odd assembly of office module fabric dividers and residential wooden cabinetry. Placing an order at the rigged-up customer counter was an act of faith.

The cooking area had too much space in the middle, a dead spot for work, a collision zone for workers. The cooking equipment, two plug-in grills, a roaster, and two microwaves, had no exhaust feature. Grease and smoke dissipated as it could, everywhere in the room. It gradually darkened all the surfaces beyond the reach of mops and sponges. The sticky blackness settled on the colored plastic glass of the new Home Depot Tiffany-style pendant chandeliers. In a kind of reverse tribute to Akron's industrial past, the grime darkened the ceiling so steadily that no one really noticed as the room got progressively gloomier.

The place definitely had something going on. It had a bounce and an energy, a heart and spirit that attracted return business. People liked the no-frills basics, the ceramic mugs of strong coffee. It was honest, authentic, and despite the difficulties, they laughed a lot in there. Its many defenders and fans forgave the deficiencies as proof of the focus on the mission.

Before they accepted the gift of the free building on Grant Street, South Street Ministries held Sunday church in the Summit Lake Community Center. The migration of Sunday worship from the community center did not change the service, but the congregation expanded. Brian Kunkler at The Chapel on The University of Akron's campus was a friend of Duane's. To young Christians struggling with the conservatism of The Chapel, Brian suggested South Street.

Single women came in greater numbers, despite the condition of the ladies' room. One of the two stalls had a shower curtain acting as a wall and a door. The sinks dispensed cold water only and the old mirror reflected something vague and sepia toned.

Though the whole place was a little uncomfortable and strange, it was safe. Lisa, with her constancy and calm insistence about certain things in the café, made vigorous cleaning a routine. It mattered that everyone had that level of welcome. The daily maintenance was an opportunity to put a mop in hand and some money in a pocket. There were the flowers on the tables, changed to reflect the season or holiday.

Whatever crazy new thing came out of Duane and the guys, there was still the tenderness of the vase. That one aspect of unnecessary tenderness held volumes of mystery. The message of love had concrete reality in Lisa's practical habits of care and homemaking. Her message was spiritually magnified on the tables. The tiny gesture of respect represented in the twisted paper autumn leaves in white vases had an electric current of connection to her culture, to her big Italian family around the kitchen table, generation after generation.

The Sunday service took on a character of a Christian dating service, a precursor to Christian Mingle, in real time and space.

The Front Porch bachelors had something new to talk about in the basement.

Anne Schillig came back to Akron from Peace Corps service and was introduced to South Street through her good friend, Hillary Stewart. Eric first saw her on a volunteer paint crew for First Glance. He knew he had to ask her out before any of the other guys realized how great she was.

On their first date, he told her how he got to South Street. He told her everything about his recent past. "I have a lying addiction, and I have to be one hundred percent truthful." Eric felt Anne deserved to know it all and make a decision about him.

They had a second date.

And then a third date.

They were one of several couples created through the Front Porch Café's early days.

On Christmas Day, 2010, two vans were idling in the basketball court in the predawn darkness of the Crabbs family front yard. Duane and Lisa stood in a circle with a large eclectic group of South Streeters, including Eric and Anne, praying for safety on the thirty-hour journey to the city of Juarez, just across the border from El Paso, Texas. Their son Joshua was working for Casas por Cristo, an organization that paired American mission groups with a local pastor to build a house for a specific family. After the five-day build, the group planned to celebrate New Year's Eve in San Antonio on the way home. As they honked their way down the challenging steep gravel driveway, Eric gripped the wheel and tried to concentrate, tried not to think about his plan.

Everyone except Anne was aware of Eric's intention to propose during the trip. Though there was some switching of occupants at the rest stops on the way, Eric and Anne never rode in the same van. The planning for the proposal gave the long drive a purpose. It was a group project they built together while building the three-room house in Juarez.

After the five-day build and discomfort of sleeping bags and minimal showering, Anne was not in the mood for a fancy New Year's Eve. The stop in San Antonio added a few more hours to the stultifying diagonal drive across the continent. Bethany was trying to talk her into the spirit, suggesting they go for a manicure downtown. Part of the elaborate diversion was instructing Anne to just do whatever Bethany wanted, as long as it kept her away from her boyfriend Matt.

Going for a manicure fit the task, so Anne joined in, for the sake of the whole group thing and for whatever Matt had in mind for Bethany. The two women traded their work boots for heels, the bandanas for spangles. It was a beautiful Texas night, and they enjoyed turning some heads as they strolled towards the Riverwalk to find their friends.

The rest of the group was waiting for them, each person with a candle and a message for Anne. Though she saw that her job was a ruse, she was not sure what was going on. Eric had not eaten any lunch at the barbeque place, which he had been looking forward to. She thought he was getting sick because he forgot and brushed his teeth with tap water.

Meanwhile, as the end of 2010 was counting down, Eric was sweating as he paced around the preset candles in the front of the Alamo, waiting for Anne to appear. He was nervous. "What if she hesitates, what if she says no? What was taking them so long? Does she know already? Am I ready? Is this a big mistake?"

Eric was prone to the negative, saw all the perils of this big dumb idea. At last he could hear them coming, hear Anne's distinctive throaty deep voice. He went down on a knee.

"Yes."

As his own fortunes and prospects were turning for the better in Akron, Eric wanted to return the trust Duane shown in him. It was not just the job, it was an entire community, and now the potential for a life, a family, with Anne.

~

Six months after Anne and Eric bought and moved into a beautiful, big, old Victorian house in Highland Square, Eric was stressed in a bundle of new ways, but work was the main source of worry. Eric, in trying to be like Jesus, feared he was merely hustling Jesus. His Duane-inspired trust in others had not gone well. Too much faith and failure gripped him in flop sweat. He gave people the benefit of the chance again and again. He suspected that the word on the street was that he was a patsy.

Eric, like all the men working in the café, had been on the game themselves. They knew how to recognize a street hustle. The café had no tolerance for intolerance. This was basic house policy, no crap talk, clearly established by Duane's approach. Witnessing Duane's reaction to being taken for a sucker was an unforgettable display of fury. Once sparked to ignite, the intensity was open to the public.

Duane was not someone with a checklist. A person could have a hundred strikes and not be out with Duane, as long as they were willing to be honest.

He did not pressure anyone into a system of recognizable goals. There was no minimum standard in the work of urban ministry. Eric knew this, knew that Duane was not judging his performance. He reminded himself that anything he did could be a reflection of Jesus. Providing a clean bathroom was a reflection of Jesus. But despite what he told himself, he wanted a win; he needed a conversion. He worked in a place that lived the rules of street hustle, and if he had to hustle Jesus, he would.

Eric knew when someone was gaming him from his own experience. He thought if he could recognize and nail the lie early enough, he could save that person from the path that his own lies had taken him. Eric recognized his real downfall was the addiction to lying. The lies, more than any other part of his descent, got him to prison. He understood the thrill of the lie.

Of the women who made the café a regular stop, Chantel stood out from the rest in the quiet deliberate way she carried herself. She was not in a rush, ever. Eric was trying to strike the right balance with the demands of some of the women, but he kept his eye on Chantel. A tall striking Black woman in her early thirties, she became a regular at the café. She lived a short walk from the café, in an apartment in an old house across from the main postal facility on Grant Street.

Eric felt bad because there was no one at the café to work with the women. Chantel was smart, interesting. They were curious about each other, and he hoped if they kept taking slow steps of trust together, maybe there was a chance for something deeper.

As they got to know each other, Chantel told Eric she had a meth habit and an older man in her life. When she needed extra money, she used the list of men she dated. She was powerful, with a strong sexual current that had a dissembling effect on men. Eric was not immune to the charm, but he turned their growing relationship to things that other men did not see—her intelligence.

He asked her to come to Sunday worship. She did. She returned the next week. She told Eric she wanted to help young girls stay out of trouble, so he invited her to a workshop. The workshop was not about helping girls, but Eric thought it could speak to Chantel. Sponsored by Reaching Above Hopelessness and Brokenness (RAHAB), a Christian ministry dedicated to the needs of prostituted women in Akron, it was about recognizing the signs of sex trafficking. As the presenter was talking about the ways young girls are targeted and groomed, Chantel left the room. Eric waited a while before he left to find her. She was out in the parking lot, crying. Chantel had never come near anything close to the vulnerability of crying in front of Eric. "That was me. I want out. I don't want the life anymore."

Eric wasted no time.

He talked to the women at RAHAB, to get their advice on what would be the best situation for Chantel, given her functional twenty years of drugs and prostitution. Chantel would need a six-month residency program. Over the next week, she stayed in the café through the day, and as he was able, Eric sat with her, both of them with their laptops open, looking for a bed in a Christian-based facility on short notice. He found a suitable small residency program for women with a range of recovery issues two hours southwest of Akron. Six months away meant she would need to give up her apartment. She agreed to go.

The plans were all in place after about a week, including the financing. Eric took her shopping to buy the bedding, towels, robe, and other items on the list sent by the program. At the same time, Eric started to feel uneasy. He suspected Chantel was using, though she denied it. On the weekend before her departure, a few volunteers helped Eric and Chantel finish up the last of the packing of her belongings. All she had left to do the night before was finish up her own packing for the residency. After she left, all her bagged and boxed belongings would go to a storage locker.

He called her from his car, not far from her apartment, around nine p.m.

She said she was home, in for the night.

When his knock on the door went unanswered, he headed down the street to the Narcotics Anonymous meeting at Community of Christ, the building next to the Front Porch Café. He spotted her in a group of people in the parking lot. Simultaneous with the recovery meeting inside, there was often a kind of reverse meeting outside, with other solutions for pain relief. Chantel was with her older gentleman, scoring drugs.

Eric took her home after the transaction. What little he said focused on the lie to him, not her behavior. She said again she was ready to go, this is what she wanted, and there were just things she had to do for the last time. She would be ready for him at ten o'clock the next day.

Eric felt a creeping doubt about the arrangements he had created. He needed help, and in a state of anxious despair as he drove home, called on a sober female friend.

She said, "If she is ready, it will work, Eric. And if she isn't ready, it is still worth it.

"I just want to have a success."

The two-hour ride south through Ohio countryside was a neutral buffer between Grant Street life and what was next. Unlike the facilities in Akron, with the potential of easy connections immediately outside the door, this place was in the middle of flat corn country, Nowheresville.

The place was completely inconspicuous, tucked behind a modest country-modern Protestant church. It gave no indication that fifteen women called it home. The pair from Akron standing in the foyer was a different demographic from the others they could see past the admitting desk. Eric was a man, and Chantel was Black. Everyone else in the place was female and white. Chantel was committing to six months with strangers with very different backgrounds. It felt like an adult Christian sleepover, a getaway for women seeking recovery from manicure addictions. The initial intake went smoothly enough, a pleasant, polite welcome in a smiling southern inflection. The last thing to go for Chantel was her cell phone. That was harder than anything else, so Eric let her have one more conversation, outside, before it went into a box.

She was outside long enough for Eric to be embarrassed and uncomfortable.

The phone surrendered; Chantel was officially on day one on the path of Christian addiction treatment. Eric was tired, felt he had done all he could, and handed it over to Christ. As he got back in his car, he felt exhausted in ways he never knew he could be exhausted. "Is this how it feels to be used up by Jesus?"

Trying to stay alert, he reverted to his negative tendencies, suspecting his desire for a success clouded his capacity to see clearly. Chantel was not really committed to getting sober, but he pushed it anyway.

Chantel found her way back to Akron the next day.

Eric was not really surprised. He realized he had operated way outside of his experience or understanding. He engineered a solution for his benefit, and Chantel had done the same. She saw an opportunity in his eagerness to take care of her loose ends, a way of cutting old ties for a restart.

The moment in the RAHAB workshop was real, he knew that. But when and if it would amount to a change for her was none of his business. It was clear to Eric that they both used each other to get what they needed. South Street had a wide arc for well-intentioned mistakes. Duane's consistent message was that it was okay to be faulty, but not false. Eric did not waste time trying to dodge his role in the misguided intervention. He found the words and spoke them out. "I realized that in this line of work, there is a lot of gaming going on, and it is always going to be a gamble. But we're playing with God's chips, not ours. It's not our decision, getting out of the game. It's not second or third chances here, it's staying in, staying on, staying with."

Eric acknowledged after Chantel that he was not the guy to help the women coming to South Street. Even when there was no physical attraction, the sexuality was hard to get around. Despite the mutual curiosity and steps they took together, he and Chantel had too much background to overcome. He, by making a conscious effort to avoid sexualizing their relationship and Chantel, suspicious that all his goodness might be just another hungry man's disguise.

He realized if he was to be of any spiritual use in the café, he had to stick with men. And there were always the men; walking out of Summit County Jail around the corner, the café was often their first stopping place. After the basics of a phone, coffee, and the bathroom, some of the guys needed more. There were the men he gave a mop and bucket to wash down the floor after the café closed. As the mop swung back and forth calmly, methodically, the man holding it, looking down, might need to just talk. Eric listened.

~

Larvett was not one to be pushed, and he had nothing to say about Eric's new business idea of starting a drive-thru service to compete with McDonald's. But they were like brothers, and Eric could tell that Larvett was intrigued. He was a thoughtful guy with big chef dreams, and Eric knew that as he put together the typical bacon and egg orders that morning, he was building a recipe for a signature South Street breakfast wrap.

Eric, following the marketing lead of street beggars, drew up a simple promotional handheld sign intended for the drivers of cars waiting at the light after coming up the exit ramp off I-77 between the café building and the McDonald's. He was going to test out an idea for another little job he could offer someone who needed lunch.

Everyone who sat down to eat was treated with the same hospitality. But if a client could not pay and was capable, he liked to have a task to give them. The café needed business, and right outside was the potential for expansion.

He went out to give it a try. Though there was someone with a sign on the northbound exit over the bridge, there was no one on the café side of the bridge, the southbound exit. He hunched up a bit in his hoodie, head covered, held the sign at chest level and smiled. Right away, a car slowed as the driver's window lowered.

"Hey, you a veteran?"

Eric nodded.

"You don't have to do that, man. They got stuff for you at the VA! Everything you need! Check it out!"

Eric did not have a chance to reply. The guy drove off without reading his sign.

I AM FINE! HOW ARE YOU? ARE YOU HUNGRY?

GOOD FOOD, CLOSE BY, AT THE FRONT PORCH CAFÉ!

Radiance

After three years of fundraising, design permits, and construction, only half the Front Porch building was renovated, but the café, the heart and soul of the place, was up and running. The aroma of eggs, bacon, and coffee filled the room once again, but the less desirable byproducts of the fryer and grill were gone, drawn off by the massive grease hood. All sparkle and shine, the full-service kitchen and dining room sparkled to oohs and aahs at the grand reopening.

I was tired and entered the café at closing time with my painting clothes and a small heap of resentment for having offered to paint the stage walls. Despite the fact that the café was making more money every day after the reopening than any day prior, there was a gloomy feeling in the room. The long wait was over. Thomas Jones, the chef, could hardly look at me. We had worked well together for so long, planning his first kitchen, and there was no joy in the man.

"Hey, Thomas, have you named her yet?" I was referring to the stove, a brand-new Radiance; six burners, flat grill, double oven, a real beauty. The former semi-kitchen had no stove. But Thomas just shrugged. Even the oven seemed forlorn. In the glum silence, I realized what was going on. I forgot what happens after the success of a building project.

I had forgotten the charged emotions of those most directly affected by the new thing. Instead of the expected satisfaction of reaching a goal, deep depression arises, a longing for what was, a state of being that is now history. The past becomes mythic.

The desire to return to what only exists as memory in the midst of what should bring joy is confusing and painful. Add to that the opinions of those not involved, but unrestrained in sharing their suggestions with you. In fact, people often feel free to make judgments that they would never consider if commenting on one of your children.

As I stood in the results of our work together, I was caught off-guard by Thomas. He, more than anyone, had been deeply invested in the details. He studied the drawings at night and would bring me suggestions and ideas to improve the plans. We looked at other restaurant kitchens together. It was my favorite part of the project, dreaming it through with Thomas. It was his kitchen; he had been the quiet steady believer, but now his silence was one of deep withdrawal. In the gleaming simple efficiency of the new commercial grade kitchen of the Front Porch Café in South Akron, Ohio, everyone seemed scared.

I changed into my painting clothes. The café was closed, and the staff was cleaning up. As I waited for my co-volunteer painter Erin Woodson to arrive, I remembered the syndrome, a thing I would describe as a "Mission Accomplished Fatigue," a singular condition that often follows the successful completion of a protracted construction project. Officially undiagnosed, its common manifestations include depression, lassitude, and fatalism. Comparable to postpartum depression in its singularity of cause, the best evocation of its effect is suggested in the Jerry Lieber and Mike Stoller song "Is That All There Is?" particularly as rendered by Peggy Lee in the 1969 recording.

I did not recognize the symptoms because I no longer suffered from a continuous loop of my own form of spatial nostalgia. After a lifetime in its grip, it was the instant decision to move to Akron that had been the start of its final round in my chemistry. It was only by the recognition of its absence that I understood the power of its hold over me. By now, three and a half years after moving to Akron, I recognized I was free of it.

My obsession with decay and the intense attachment to lost places may be typical of those who experience unexplained sudden catastrophic loss as children. But my freedom from its hold was new, and I was hesitant to examine it, as though doing so would snatch me back into its grip. My relation to the freedom felt like a newly fallen giant tree, with the exposed circle of earth and roots still dripping sap. Squirrels and birds plummet to the earth in the absence of its branches. I could only whisper and tiptoe towards such silent power now stilled.

The ceaseless longing for gone or dying places was some substitute, some shape for the barbed chains on my physical heart. I could barely move at times when in places that connected with incomprehensible feelings of sadness. There were so many of them, so many swerves needed to avoid them. Architecture became a focus to avoid the obsession with decay, with past places. I loved change because it could seem to obliterate the sadness of past structures.

As Gary hypnotically moved the mop across the floor, I listened to his unexpected pained confusion. My painting clothes were not so different than my architect clothes, really, but the body in the clothes was no longer the cheerleader of the past three years. Simple listening was all that was needed, not my previous rousing assurances of eventual success. We had done it. It was time for presence, for stillness, for attending.

It had taken twice as long and twice as much effort to renovate half the space of their building. The old building had a lot of issues, as did its owner. Yes, we were special. While new construction is easier to regulate, old buildings require modifications and variances. Our paper trail brought us to the Summit County Building Department so many times, they had a special name for the project. They called the building the Front Porch Crapé. But while the structure itself was unremarkable, and unlovable by the Building Department, its lack of great bones was offset by a rich history and association for a lot of people.

The café is the day-to-day expression of South Street Ministries. Staffed by ex-offenders, it's an informal living room for its neighborhood in South Akron. After hours, the space hosts meetings of twelve-step recovery groups, reentry programs, an international dinner, and occasional theatricals.

I kept listening; Gary and his mop, David and the dishes, Thomas and the stove, all the while my painting time was dwindling. Erin Woodson and I had to finish up before the women's AA meeting at six o'clock. But I knew that the more important task was to listen. Gary and Thomas were afraid that the café would change, that people who felt unwelcome in other places but get a smile and a seat at the café would feel edged out by a new clientele. They were afraid that things would be different.

~

We had very little time for our stage painting session. The big percolator was on the corner table, in preparation for the AA meeting. Erin started cutting in as I freed the corners of the stage from the miscellaneous stuff that landed there during the renovation. The stage was not original to the 1920s building. Originally a grocery store, it was converted into the Croatian American Club in the 1940s. It is easy to imagine a band on that stage for the weddings, baptisms, first communions, anniversaries. But for a host of reasons, it no longer invites performance or church use. It feels too high, too removed from the rest of the room. Preaching, lectures, poetry readings, plays and music   all happen closer, in front of the stage.

I moved the loose odd stuff, as well as the piano that never gets played and the droopily angled-fringed-eagled-dusty American flag to the center of the stage and covered them, becoming progressively downcast at the condition of the existing walls. They needed more than a coat of paint. Fetching the closest source of spackle would take at least twenty minutes round trip. We barely had enough time as it was to maneuver the paint around the tight pile in the center of the stage. Something else would have to work.

I took off my shoes, stood on the piano bench, and started rolling. After laying in half a wall, I could see that one coat of the pale blue paint over the existing beige gave the effect of clouds. From a distance, it suggested a dappled sky, enough to disguise the cracks and dings. It was a stage after all. A bit of innocuous scenic detail could not offend anyone.

Erin painted along the corners, out of sight on the far side of the covered mound. A few months prior, we had both been part of a gang of irregulars on a road trip led by Duane and Lisa. South Street is a member of the Christian Community Development Association (CCDA), and we had driven together to Memphis for the annual convention.

I fell into the rhythm of the paint roller. On opposite sides of the stage as we worked, I felt a kind of shared intimacy. I called over the pile between us. "Hey, Erin, did you and Bobbie fall for each other in Memphis?"

Erin was prone to laughter, and that was her answer. They had recently announced they were a couple.

We chatted a bit before the sound of the roller took over in our effort to finish quickly.

My memories of Memphis shared something with Bobbie and Erin's romance; the ending of one thing and the beginning of another. The Memphis Convention Center was close to the National Civil Rights Museum at the Lorraine Motel, and the entire South Street group of fifteen decided to walk to the museum together. The glue of our wildly diverse and jovial group, ambling down a recreated pedestrian version of Main Street was just that—a joy of moving discovery and appreciation of our company. We were unguarded, visitors in another culture, enjoying an unstructured afternoon in a city with a different story. On one level it was a freeing feeling, this walk through a time-stamped version of Memphis. The streetcars rolled by, bells ringing, but the heritage felt preserved and frozen while we, the tourists, were the live moving parts of the picture. We gave it the odd bounce of real.

I carried a mix of dread as we moved closer. Of the fifteen people from South Street, only five were alive when Martin Luther King was assassinated in Memphis after addressing striking sanitation workers. I was one of only three old enough to remember the events of April 1968. I walked with forty years respectful distance from a tragedy I felt unworthy to mourn, without access to understanding why. Towards the Lorraine Motel, I carried a murky unexamined complicity; my whiteness and something more personal but equally murky—the perpetual dark mystery around my father's violent death, five years before King, when I was seven years old.

My father's homicide was mysterious. Suddenly gone, his life itself was then erased. If any part of him was discussed, it never happened in my presence, unless whispered furtively by others, close to the ear of others, between people outside our family.

There was no language for this man, my father, only the scattered, shattered bits of his existence slowly drifting down on his family as a blanket of dull gray dust.

Five years later, Reverend King's assassination came in the midst of upheaval in the United States. His path of nonviolence made him an early critic of the Vietnam War. He gave me an image I could hold secretly, in the absence of my own father. But it was secret because he was a hero, and I did not deserve a hero.

The black and white vision of the balcony where King lay after the shooting is an image stomped on the soul. As we came to the building, it felt that there were not enough sunglasses in the world to stop the condemning glare coming off that balcony.

Inside the museum, the carpet cleaner smell, the low lights, the recorded sounds and exhibits felt oppressive, a carnival show. I quietly turned away from the group and went outside. Whatever was going on with me, I didn't want to make the afternoon about me. The whole thing brushed too close to the confusion around my own story. The story in the museum was pain, a redemptive pain. My pain was illegitimate, not allowed, no redemption here. Whether it was a false panic or not, it felt too much like drowning.

I walked all around the neighborhood surrounding the museum to calm down. The converted industrial lofts gave off a trendy, gentrified feel, enhancing the disconnection of the preserved facade of the motel. I sat with Jacqueline Smith for a while. She was the last resident of the motel, forcibly evicted and for the twenty-seven years since, has been protesting what she sees as a travesty of Dr. King's message. From a legally mandated distance from the museum, she urges people not to buy tickets, says the motel could be put to better use. With the ticket I bought burning in my pocket, I asked her if there was something I could do with my money instead. When she recommended a Black-owned bakery a few blocks away, I ran there, carrying back boxes of cookies, trying to outrun and outspend the feeling, but it wouldn't shake.

Across the street from the Lorraine Motel Building, the state had acquired the rooming house where James Earl Ray had waited with a rifle. I was curious as an architect how the building worked as a museum, how a visitor was taken through that material.

The investigation photos, court transcripts, clothing, and the rifle itself blur in my memory against the shock of the final display. At the end of a hall on the top floor, behind thick Plexiglas, is a perfectly preserved dingy bathroom, the small single window slightly open. The view is still the same, perfectly preserved, a direct line to the balcony.

The last thing in the experience is James Earl Ray's point of view through the scope of a rifle. The last thing a visitor sees at the National Civil Rights Museum is the view of a man who shot Martin Luther King.

The killers had the last word.

It was so cold and lonely.

I ran down the emergency stairs and outside.

"Mary! Over here!" I heard Cheryl Tucker before I saw her sitting on a low wall and ran to her. We hugged, relieved to be outside, to find each other.

Cheryl and I had relocated to Akron at the same time. We had different explanations for landing in Akron but shared the same immigration fundamentals: we were mature women needing to step away from our lives to go alone to a new place, to make something new of ourselves.

When you have the willingness or the necessity to leave the life you know for something you don't, strange things can happen. Neither of us would have imagined ourselves living in an intentional group house in our fifties. But the unlikely domestic arrangement gave us a place for our friendship to begin.

Now here we were, side by side, dripping with emotion, from two different sides of the story told inside the museum and beating everywhere else today out of our foundational American racial history.

"Those pictures, the women, that could be my grandmother." She barely got the words out. Neither of us was capable of articulating our distress. We were just relieved to find each other, to catch our breath together, to sit on that bench together in the warmth of an October afternoon. That was the way out, just sitting together, waiting for the rest of our friends, looking forward to walking back down Main Street, finding a spot for a meal together.

~

Erin and I continued to work silently around the stage. Working the roller around Erin's corners, I wondered if she was thinking about her Memphis story. I recognized that Memphis had loosened up the ties around forbidden grief. I knew the outline of Cheryl's history, and she knew mine. We found each other through South Street, and we found each other again in the deeper space of the unspoken blessing of that bench together.

On Sunday, our last morning in Memphis, we went for breakfast before the drive back to Akron. Thomas picked the restaurant, always interested to see how a good local place ran the kitchen. The restaurant was not expecting a crowd of fifteen, and it was clear that it would take a long time to get food to the table. We got on our feet, sharing aprons, passing out menus, serving, bussing tables, making the most of the unexpected turn. In typical South Street fashion, it was God's time.

At our long table, breakfast became a party, with Duane and Lisa hosting a few extra visitors as well. The cars parked outside would get us home when it was time to go.

Remembering Bobby's unlikely role as a server, I tried again. "Erin, was it at the café there? Sunday morning, the endless breakfast? Bob waiting on customers? That was so much fun."

Again, she laughed.

Erin was able to do most of the cutting before six p.m., our deadline, but I had a long way to go on the walls. Erin left, and I asked the chairwoman of the AA meeting if I could keep working. Reassuring her that it was quiet work, I also told her I was in recovery, and it would be nice to just listen as I finished painting. The recovery meetings had just returned to the café after a three-month absence during the renovation. From around the corner of the stage, I heard a woman tell the others about the new bathroom.

"Yeah, nice mirror, too," someone else added.

For a moment I thought of stepping out and introducing myself as the architect. Instead, I keep the steady, quiet rhythm of the roller, suggesting clouds on stage walls.

I had expected to be long gone from Akron by now, but here I was, painting to the accompaniment of an AA meeting in this place I had come to love. What had become a mission of service for me had evolved into the embrace of a community.

Duane had the gift of making people, of making me, feel special. He listened, he asked questions, he was present.

Lisa had perhaps the rarer gift. She made me feel like I belonged. No, not that, not just feeling. You really did belong with Lisa. It was a palpable real sensation for those of us who mostly feel judged, unworthy, dismissed, or marginalized. Because it can be subtle, such attitudes, the complete absence of that with Lisa stands out. Lisa makes me feel like one of the girls.

When the meeting was over, I joined in for the closing circle and prayer and thanked them. I finished up the painting. I cleaned up the brushes in the mop sink in the dish room, happy to have the task done. Memphis reminded me that the wounds I believe keep me apart are exactly what finally bring me in; the wounds we protect as unique are the wounds we share when we are ready to join in. I don't have to cut myself out of the picture, out of the circle of hands clasping hands. South Street gave me that confidence. I stood back from the work we did. It was good; it was what it needed to be. I walked through the kitchen, stopping in front of the Radiance stove. "Thomas. That is your name."

Of course. It was his kitchen, his stove.

I turned back to look at the place as I turned off the lights, catching the gleam off the Radiance, off Thomas, before the room went to shadow.

III

The Holy See

The city is ringed in green ridges breeched by the Cuyahoga River
valley winding against and below street level. One enters downtown
by the anonymous ferocity of expressways, or by the graceful Y Bridge
arcing over the river. Akron, exalted place.

"I just don't think homosexuality is in God's plan."

Pastor Duane Crabbs made this pronouncement as he attempted to stand out of the compressed, sagging lounge chair on the raised platform at the back of Angel Falls Coffee Shop in Highland Square, Akron, Ohio on Thursday, June 6, 2013.

For the previous four months, we met weekly for conversation at the popular coffee shop. We were working on a book project about the history of South Street Ministries, the organization he founded in partnership with his wife, Lisa.

I aimed for nonchalance as we worked our way vertical from the low-slung upholstery. There was no way around the simple declaration. I knew we had differing views on the subject, but his blunt statement about homosexuality, about me, to me, silenced me. I shifted to a neutral stance, my normal public posture to dismissive statements.

Typical of Duane, a man who lives in the present moment, he had already started talking to the two people clutching open laptops poised to occupy the seats we had just vacated. Thus freed from responding to his comment, I was simultaneously shutting down. Duane had exposed the limits to which I could trust him. My demeanor betrayed nothing of the internal process of backing away slowly, stealthily, towards the back door, seeing the defining limits on the friendship. He was becoming a fixed thing now, an object in my diminishing gaze. I had not set a trap for him; he found it on his own. He was a homophobe.

Those who occupy minority status, in this case my minority, homosexuals, must always contend with the assumptions of the majority. Any kind of minority will be outside the common standard of the larger group, the majority. Therefore, the minority has the gift of seeing and understanding those assumptions that the majority cannot. The majority is reinforced in its view of the world because those values are the common qualities of the crowd. This leads to a more adaptive capacity in the minority; multilingual, they understand the nuance of the majority class but communicate with each other in the minority patois.

This imbalance, this reality, has no intrinsic moral value. It's normal. However, human beings in a majority caste can trend towards suspicion and control over the minority. Picking up the offhand remark is a necessary survival skill for the minority. Such recognition allows the prey to elude the predator. I took it in and gave away nothing, closing up without a hint, assuming the familiar cool face over the vulnerable body.

Duane's pronouncement about God's plan not including homosexuals came at a moment in my personal evolution which allowed for a more nuanced response. While my first inclination was to shut the door on any deeper potential for our relationship, I stopped the door as it was closing. I held it, paused, gave space for something else to enter.

I recognized that Duane was the one struggling with something here, not me. My only legitimate reaction to his statement was disappointment— nothing in my legal or personal life was remotely threatened by his words. Though in his theology he had essentially just banished me from belonging and made me other, I knew him too well to dismiss him as a homophobe, a word that is itself harsh and dismissive. He was not my enemy.

This was an opportunity to respond with love. My historic plan of action, removing my heart from the relationship, would be cowardly and lazy. I understood by now that I was not in Akron to build buildings. My work was bridges. Indignation was a righteous fiction, and the boring expected option compared to the potential for truth and growth.

I took a different course with Duane. He was the one troubled by his indictment, not me. I let him know if there was anything I could do to help in his struggle, I was available. There was no hesitation in this trust because I knew that he was devoted to those on the margins. I recognized that he, as an Evangelical Christian, had the potential to help others on both sides of the issue. He had created an environment of safety, a place that was genuine in welcoming all—in particular those who were otherwise dismissed. If I could be his companion to widen the embrace of the broken souls that find their way to South Street Ministries, what greater service could I render?

Duane is a man true to his own history while continually building relationships with struggling people. He responds to needs as they arise, willing to bear the discomfort and sorrow of the needy and meet the level of pain with his compassion and exposure.

Prior to his pastoral work, he was an urban firefighter and paramedic. There is no space for discrimination in emergency response. As a pastor, he operates on that same response reflex—triage—the first focus is given to the highest and most immediate need. He moves forward not by the exterior picture, but is drawn by the heat of the beating, bleeding sacred heart of any person. He moves aside the obstacles of issues or barriers to stand with the individual.

In the early 1980s, when the mechanism for transmission of Acquired Immune Deficiency Syndrome (AIDS) was still unknown, becoming infected was a death sentence. As a paramedic in Cleveland at that time, Duane cared for many early AIDS patients. As a first line responder, Duane would routinely handle people suffering from opportunistic diseases preying on the bodies of people with collapsed immune systems. Many health care professionals routinely refused to touch such patients, fearing any exposure to what was a mysterious plague.

Gloves and masks were not mandatory at the time. Emergency responses can be chaotic and unpredictable, with close contact between victims and EMS workers. Duane incurred an accidental needle stick that required an HIV test. His results were negative for the virus; he was not infected with AIDS.

Duane was not a patronizing Christian around gay people. He was not the type who "love the sinner, hate the sin," a particularly irritating form of shaming. I had already chosen silence a few times when Duane made an insensitive comment. It was time to let him know as he spoke that there is no such thing as "a gay lifestyle."

I couldn't walk away. We had a strong net of connections by this point.

First, we were solid. We were friends. We loved each other.

Second, he was my client. We were planning the renovation of the Front Porch building. He and his wife Lisa had created South Street Ministries sixteen years earlier from the house they moved into with their four children. Steadily the ministry had grown from their house to the point where they had been given a building. I was an architect looking for a project that reflected my social conscience. They had a building with needs. They did not ask me; I chose them. In a reversal of normal practice, I picked them as my client. I just knew it was what I was meant to do. I moved to Akron from New York City on the strength of a weekend visit.

Third, we had entertained an audience at the Akron Art Museum with our unlikely partnership. The museum invited Duane to participate in an experiment they called Slide Jam. We were the last presenters in what turned out to be a much longer event than anticipated. But we revived the attention of the weary audience. Duane and I had the theatrical tension of contradiction, the suspense of opposites and a powerful message. We could laugh together about the stereotype of our story as the common grist of daytime talk shows: "The story of the New York lesbian architect and the storefront evangelical pastor finding common ground in Akron, Ohio."

Fourth, Duane and I were the Akron representatives on the Spiritual Committee for the Gay Games. Modeled on the Olympics, the sports and cultural festival is held every four years in a different international city and is open to all adult participants. In 2014, Northeast Ohio hosted. Every month for the nine months leading up to the events of August 2014, we drove to the Gay and Lesbian Center in Cleveland to meet with participating, supportive clergy. I was designing the spiritual space for the Gay Games

Olympic Village. At those meetings, Duane never exhibited the common response of a straight man who finds himself in a room of gay men—he was completely himself, neither threatened nor flattered by ordinary interaction with men who also happened to be homosexual.

Any one of those first four truths was enough for me to choose a loving response over a protective reaction. But beyond those existing conditions, the most compelling force keeping me open despite Duane's offhand dismissive remark was as yet unknown to me. I decided to be his ambassador to my culture because I thought I owed it to him as a friend. I thought I was in control here. I did not know I was orchestrating the conditions for the third time Akron would save my life.

Our relationship stayed as easy as it had been. We were never formal in discussing homosexuality, we never consulted the "clobber passages" in the Bible. There was no focus group. There remained plenty of small points we saw differently about the God/homosexuality question, but if anything, our appreciation of each other and trust through those differences only grew deeper.

~

In the fall of that year, Duane asked me to share my story after he gave the Sunday message at South Street. Up to this point, he had never expressed a public position on the divisive issues of abortion and homosexuality. He resisted being in someone else's category. But he was prepared to address one of the two "Third Rail" issues. When he asked if I would be willing to say something about my experience, I simply said yes. I trust the heart of this unusual man. Besides, I thought I was steering the ship, so it was a pleasure to be of service. I had not the slightest suspicion of what was ahead.

The Front Porch Café was church on Sunday. The renovation was moving slowly, as the modest fundraising efforts took shape. "Everybody deserves good design" had become my operating philosophy, but building that philosophy was another matter. Resources were slim. The money for the renovation came slowly. South Street Ministries never passed a basket or appealed for contributions from those who came to the services on Sunday.

Up to this point all I had designed was the handicapped entry ramp at the side parking lot and the new front entry door. But even the two small changes made a big impact. The handicapped ramp made it easier for people to come in. The clear glass storefront entry door with a customized teak wood handle replaced a blank solid steel door. The new door gave a completely different feeling to entering the building. Just the simplicity of the human hand touching wood, the free light passing into the interior was uplifting. It graced the act of entry and changed people's posture from defensive to the expectation of welcome.

At first, I came to church in a professional sense, to understand the needs of the place, to translate the hopes of the community to the concrete reality of the physical building. Sitting through the evangelical Jesus-focused messages, I was introduced to the beauty, lyricism, and poetry of the Bible. Growing up Catholic, I was never encouraged to read the Bible. My ignorance was magnified by fear after a number of direct confrontations by Bible-waving zealots.

I was strangely receptive to what was happening in that room. I liked being among people who interpreted things differently than I did. We were all facing the same direction. I let go of the need to feel like the smartest person in the room and listened. There was something going on in that modest brick two-story in a neighborhood that had seen better days.

I fell in with the format for worship at South Street Ministries. Starting twenty minutes after the designated time is routine. Beforehand, socializing and milling about is normal. The café setup encourages such interaction. At a certain point, Toni and Cynethia step up to the front to lead singing with the accompanying recorded music, generally confined to the same three upbeat contemporary Christian Gospel songs. This is followed by Open Worship, a time when people can share something of their joys or sorrows with everyone. The assembly is witness and participant in these shares and joins in prayers for the person so sharing. Duane gives the message and sometimes there is communion.

It can be very lively in the room. The building is in the midst of human commerce—the county jail, the men's and the women's correctional facilities, the Plasma Center, halfway houses, rooming houses, and the student ghetto for The University of Akron. Lots of people who would not feel comfortable in other churches come to South Street.

Duane as a pastor never takes advantage of the emotions displayed in church. It is just a very mixed group and many things could—and do—happen. While not straying from its evangelical nature, it was spontaneous, real, and emotional, but with the leadership of Duane, never manipulative of the vulnerability so often present on a Sunday at South Street.

The regularity of the service, the coffee, the giant bag of donated bread and muffins Joe Heindel picks up every Sunday, and the genuine, real, nonjudgmental nature of the place drew people from all social and religious groups in Akron and beyond. Duane is an incredible presence on his feet, starting with his prepared message and going where it takes him. Attending had given me a new lens for my own beliefs. I found myself capable of participating fully while grounded and growing in a different theology—a growing understanding and appreciation for the mystic tradition within the Roman Catholic Church.

His message that particular Sunday began with statistics. Numbers and percentages around all kinds of sexual crime and misbehavior were brought forth. It was dry and rambling, so his point unclear. After what seemed a phone book's worth of basic terrible numbers about pornography, sex trafficking, prostitution, child sexual abuse and predatory acts, he stopped.

"And Christian Evangelicals raised thirty-nine million dollars to support Proposition 8 in California.[9] What could that same money have done if we had applied it to any of those other issues? It's just not that important. *The world has moved on.*"

Duane beckoned me and Ben to come up front to tell our stories. Ben is a tall, slim young man. His chiseled face is dominated by his beautiful big smile, so wide his eyes crinkle down to meet the smile below. Ben accepts that he is gay and has chosen a celibate life based on his religious beliefs. He presents a comfortable, happy demeanor with his decision.

My story is different, but I felt confident and relaxed facing the crowd. I knew these people, they knew me. I wanted them to feel as comfortable as I was, while not avoiding my truth. "The thing you should know is that homosexuality is not a choice. Why would anyone take a path that includes alienation from family, contempt, and physical danger? Not me! I tried to be straight. But it was not me, and so I made lousy choices. I had no barometer. Once I gave that up, I could finally grow. Being different from the majority this way is natural for about ten to fifteen percent of living things. God made us this way, so how could it be wrong? I think it's wrong not to live into this mysterious gift of God's intention."

As Ben and I spoke, there were some people who got up and left. However, comings and goings were common at South Street. People got up for coffee and sweet rolls. Others came in just for the coffee and sweet rolls. Others went out for a smoke. Mark White could participate fully while busy at all times either rolling a cigarette or in the process of traveling to light up. He once came back to his seat carrying a large pizza. I tried not to assume anything. Aside from that, it seemed to me that the room progressively settled and quieted as we spoke.

Complete silence.

Quiet intervals were a part of South Street. During open worship, there was a communal silence of encouragement. Such stillness was a pact of encouragement for the next person brave enough to walk up front in trust with their troubles or joys, their tears and now and then, their song or their poem.

But this was an uncomfortable silence. Long.

Duane invited questions.

Kim T. Jones raised her hand.

"Mary, you said something about shame. What did you mean?"

I did not consider what might be motivating Kim to ask such a question. I heard but did not register the unusual tremulous sound in her voice as she asked. Kim T. Jones was not shy, did not shrink from letting anyone know how she felt about a matter. She was a force field, a strong, Black woman belted with the Lord who brought her over from the rough side of life.

I was happy the silence was broken, happy to have an answer, moving, rushing there as I noticed but ignored Kim's uncharacteristically subdued tone.

I had a perfect example for Kim's question about shame. I did not stop to think of where I was going. Something had just happened that fit her question perfectly. I was ready with a response, ready to be helpful, and taking a pause did not occur to me. I was, in that moment, that hyperactive third-grade me, middle row, last seat, arm shooting straight up, straining the seams of my plaid uniform trying to get the attention of my teacher, Sister Claudette. I knew the answer. Call on me.

I took a breath, looking at Eric, who was standing in the back of the room. I took a step closer to everyone.

"Well, you all know Eric, that tall guy back there with the awesome beard, right? And you all know that he and Anne recently had their first baby, right? Well, I can tell you something about shame. Now, I grew up Catholic. In my day, we Catholics all had a lot of shame heaped on us. We all had what were called 'impure thoughts,' turning our souls from purity to decay.

"But for reasons I could not understand, my stuff, my dark shade, was a little different… grittier, heavier, permanent. I just accepted that I was a bad person. Those were the messages I got from my church and from the community.

"The sin part got better when I realized I was gay. It got better because I was not alone, I was not the only person who ever lived who had those feelings. So even if my church cast me in sin and denied me Communion for being who I was, I could make the decision to leave them. I could walk away from the Communion I was excluded from for being who I was.

"And I worked and walked my way into a great life. But still… there were things I did not really recognize or understand. Like when my friends and siblings started families. I felt I needed to be careful around their children. Not just in the normal, protective way, you know, from outside threats or danger. It was like I had to protect them from—me. I had to be extra-perfect, even with my own sisters' and brothers' kids.

"I just felt I had to be that way. I never really knew or questioned why. It meant I never got genuinely close to my nieces and nephews and my friend's children because I was never truly myself. I was too busy performing, too busy looking good.

"But I gotta tell you, those kids all had a great time. I was definitely the fun aunt.

"When I decided to move to Akron from New York to work with South Street, Anne and Eric invited me to rent the third floor of their house in

Highland Square. We painted the house together that summer, caulked all the windows, and shared just about everything. Despite the age difference, we were close friends. They knew I was gay; it was not an issue.

"But when Anne and Eric got pregnant, I started planning to move out. I thought I had a lot of good reasons. I was busy; I worked from home. How could I do that with a baby crying? I planned the move and had not said a word to them.

"But I knew there was something not right about what I was doing. It felt like an old pattern. I was running away from…something. So I reached out for advice. Who did I call? I chose the one person I thought most likely to agree with me. I called Anne's mother, the soon-to-be-grandmother to their child.

"Anne's mother, Sue, took a pause after I explained my situation and asked her opinion. She said, 'Why would you do a thing like that?'

"It was her question, yes, but more so the tone of her voice that took me by surprise. She sounded... bewildered, heartbroken that I would be cutting myself from the opportunity to share with family. I had expected confirmation, and instead I got… something else.

"In that something else, I finally got it. Just like that I realized what all that careful behavior around children was really all about.

"I felt I had to leave, to slip out the door in the middle of the night without telling.

"Why? Why would I choose self-banishment? I realized that even if I was extra good, it was no use. I had to leave before I fell in love with that baby.

"I had to go first. I had to leave because one day they would ask me to leave when they found out I was a filthy, child-molesting lesbian."

I stopped, suddenly silent, done. I laid a trap for myself and stepped right in. I tricked myself into a confession for a sin of which I was perfectly innocent. To hear myself say it aloud gave me a long hall of mirrors picture of my whole life in a single flash. In the shock wave that followed, I stood in expectation of a stoning. I felt I could be eliminated, destroyed, stomped out by the mob. But that feeling of extreme danger endured only for a moment, only long enough for me to know it was all a lie. My eyes, freshly opened, saw not a mob, but a beloved community witnessing my own liberation.

It was a view from the end of something, a perspective possible when we dare to turn around and see the past in a completely new light. All those years, bound by a myth not of my making, but one imposed on my family, suddenly gone.

In the concrete immediacy of such sharing, a stone is cracked open, discoveries are made. The nakedness of shame gives its opposite a birthright. The intensity of that bonding moment is so powerful it never comes undone. That is what happened to us in the room, in that place, on that day. There was not one person in that room who did not identify with my shame. It may not have been their shame, but it spoke to their own terrible burden. The burden of institutionalized or generational—or both—shame of a deep intractable shade. Shame of poverty, skin color, incarceration, abuse, addiction, wealth, persecution. As Duane said, the world had moved on. So could we.

As Kim said to me later, "You spoke your truth. There's no unsaying your truth once you speak it."

I was free to join the world as myself and move on.

The exposure in the café tripped a deeper liberation. It cracked the shame I absorbed at seven from the unspoken judgment around my family. As a child, the silent scorn manifested in strange ways—suddenly, mysteriously, and angrily, an adult was calling me dirty, a neighborhood friend could no longer play with me.

The aftereffect of my father's homicide was a silence that rendered his memory off limits to me, the youngest, with few memories of the unspoken man. It was radioactive. The story became what people around our family believed happened, and what I absorbed: that he deserved to die; that we deserved being deprived of knowing who was responsible; that the less said about the entire affair, or him the better. There was no place for him or his memory.

My freedom from unrecognized shame turns all that inside out. I claim my own story, I cherish and love the tenacity and bravery of my family, and I place my lonely father in the middle of the life around me. I take him everywhere.

I proclaim the sacredness in the profane.

Old South Main Street

Main Street implies something at the center of it all, an American cultural touchstone. A road designated as Main Street is grounded in our evolved sense of place. There is a certain kind of safety that stubbornly persists in that concept, a generally available vision of a shared idea.

Places that have grown beyond the small-town evocation of a Main Street are often renamed in attempts to infuse new life into dormant zones. Such arteries are often named after civic leaders or catchy urban planning buzzwords. They might be called "Market Place" and converted to serpentine pedestrian-only zones.

By 2017, the historic spine in the central downtown section of Akron's Main Street displayed its history and its promise in a comprehensible mile's worth of contradiction. Old commercial storefronts, more often than not displaying only reflections of the sparse pedestrian traffic, vie with block-wide planned projects. Clunky whimsical street furniture sprouted on sidewalks, outnumbering the people available to sit in them.

A snippet of Main Street was ceremoniously designated LeBron James Way. Fortunately, the street never suffered the indignity of transformation to a pedestrian-only thoroughfare. That popular well-intentioned approach to enliven downtowns more often accelerates their commercial demise. In Akron, though the storefronts may be empty, their story is very much alive in the quantity of old buildings still standing. There is a pulse that offers a promise of new life. It deserves to be called Main Street.

The particulars of this story, however, are located further along this artery.

Main Street takes on a boulevard grandeur while passing south through the monolithic brick complex of buildings that had been the B. F. Goodrich Company. But it unceremoniously and abruptly concludes at a complex of condominiums that aggressively turn their back to the street. A sharp left followed by a sharp right brings the motorist back to South Main, suddenly now a one-way artery. Any sense of civic pride is now stripped away. After that sharp right, a driver's inclination is to step on the gas, to accelerate along this corridor away from town.

A one-way street in a smaller city is created for the benefit of those who daily come in and out of that city. A one-way street is antithetical to a Main Street, to the pulse of commerce and activity. A one-way street is not what Walt Disney had in mind when he recreated Main Street USA as the gateway for the Magic Kingdom. A one-way street is made for speed and ease from here to there.

This one-way, mile-long chunk of South Main Street had been the interface between the factories and the working-class neighborhood those factories sustained. The commercial life of the street evolved into a mash-up of consumer and light industrial support businesses and a lot of bars. Transitional more than destination, it was the linking route between two defining Akron institutions, the Goodrich and the Firestone factories. At the southern end of this stretch, Main Street bridges the railroad tracks and enters Firestone territory.

This is the South Main Street for the physical grounding point of this story. This is the eastern edge of the Summit Lake neighborhood, the fifty-eight blocks of Duane and Lisa's ministry of presence.

In 1997, when the family moved to the neighborhood, Duane talked a lot about the fourteen bars and fourteen churches and the need to bring the two together. In a curious paradox that he will acknowledge, one of his early successes, the Summit Lake Faith-Based Community Alliance, may have been a major unanticipated factor in South Main's current destruction.

The Crabbs family had been living in Summit Lake for a little more than a year when Duane organized the Summit Lake Faith-Based Community Alliance. In addition to the church leaders in the group, there were also street preachers, businesspeople, and bar owners. Like Duane, the other members lived and worked in Summit Lake, and were intimately familiar with the struggles of the seven thousand people living in the old neighborhood.

At the same time, the Department of Human Services was exploring options for a satellite office in the neighborhood. Their surveys revealed that sixty percent of the families subject to losing their benefits from the overhaul of the state welfare system lived within a three-block radius of a city-owned building at 1102 South Main Street, a former BancOne annex. Out of that percentage, 650 families lived in the immediate neighborhood.

The Alliance was encouraged by that interest and proposed additional programming for the building. To offset the tide of deterioration they knew firsthand, they envisioned a day care center, outreach services, and a culinary training school. Duane wrote to the Deputy Mayor for Economic Development, James Phelps, and the Planning Director Warren Woolford, on behalf of the Alliance's interest in the building, but received no response.

Soon enough, the city had an answer. In alignment with Mayor Don Plusquellic's vision, the building was demolished on May 17. The administration saw Old South Main as the spine of a new industrial parkway between the Goodrich and Firestone campuses. The BancOne annex was the first of several buildings eliminated to prepare for unspecified development.

The demoralization of invisibility was made visible in the ghost outline of the building. In the shocked blinks of those looking at the brick-strewn emptiness, it seemed a dramatic answer to their efforts—their hopes did not matter. They stared into the gap that only the day before had been solid, a manifestation of their capacity for hope. These were people who lived within walking distance of the building, who remembered walking to a Main Street that not so long ago included butcher shops and drug stores.

The City saw revitalization in starting over by encouraging new industry in a strategic location, close to downtown and other established successful industries. Within their plan, there was not a mechanism to discuss other visions for the street. The mayor did not understand why the Alliance was against his plan, something that would make room for new things by "trying to get rid of the crap and get something new in there." The residents saw the situation differently. They were not interested in selling their houses back to the city.

The development might eventually bring the jobs and vitality the city effused about, but in the meantime, it had deepened local distrust of those trying to engage with an administration's promises and power. The building they pinned a hope on had been eliminated by those who did not take the time to listen.

A year later, Patrick Armour and Duane stood together among a large group listening to a band playing gospel at the 100th Anniversary celebration of Miller Avenue Church. Patrick saw Mayor Plusquellic standing alone and urged Duane to welcome him. Duane was reluctant, but Patrick persisted, pointing out that this was Duane's neighborhood, and the mayor was his guest.

Witnesses differ on what they heard, but everyone remembers it as a hostile encounter. The two men shared a tendency for in-your-face confrontation, to holding their ground, to making the other guy back down. Duane had publicly opposed the mayor's ideas for the neighborhood. Both men planted their heels and egos down in the midst of a church picnic. After a feisty exchange over what had happened the year before, there was a tense standoff until the mayor's phone gave him the opportunity to move, to step out of the tension.

As the band moved on to a version of "I Can See Clearly Now," Duane remembers watching the mayor hurry to his car without a backward glance. It seemed to the people who lived there that the mayor never glanced at Summit Lake again.

As of January 2017, nearly all of what had existed on that stretch was completely gone. Not only the buildings, but not a bush, tree, or streetlamp dotted the landscape. There was nothing to soften the blunt-force trauma operating daily on the street. The final stroke for the evolutionary disappearance of this part of South Main, for the eradication of everything including the natural terrain, was the redesign of access to Interstate 76. Billed as the new gateway to downtown, the dangerous exit and access ramps were pulverized into dirt in favor of an acre-devouring roundabout, sized for automobiles decelerating from sixty-five to thirty miles an hour.

Without a few landmarks, it was hard to find the functioning streets intersecting South Main, even for those living in the neighborhood. Everything was bald and flat, interrupted here and there with colossal heaps of dirt.

~

For twenty years, Duane Crabbs had worked his way into the neighborhood through the street. In his early years, he walked. At any time of day or night, the rhythm of his feet brought him into the life and people of the neighborhood. His sensitivity was tuned to people. The sincerity, desire, and capacity to connect stayed with him through the years. He remained the optimist because he stayed in the present moment. The firefighter moves into the heat, responds to the need at hand. Despite tragedies and losses he guided people through, Duane carried hope energy on the walk into the difficult. His question was not "What would Jesus do?" but "What would Jesus do if he were Duane Crabbs?"

That question gave an allowance for the range of his personality—including the unforgettable fury to those on the receiving end. Heat seeks heat, and Duane's anger when provoked had a searing immediacy. Grown men cried. That volatility was on call during his education in the working system of "street." It was his grounding education into the lives of a segment of his community. In the early years of his ministry, after nights of his walking street presence, he would end up after hours at the Main Event, a bar at the corner of Crosier and Main. His friend Claudia was the owner and barmaid there, back when bars still had barmaids.

As had become customary on the nights Duane was present, Claudia would grab the remote control and turn off the jukebox. To the protesting of the dancers, Claudia would call out, "Hey, everyone shut the fuck up. The preacher is leaving, and I want him to pray for this goddamned place."

In the confused silence, the attention would turn to Duane, some hats would be removed, some heads would bow, and some bikers' do-rags would come off.

In the early days in neighborhood bars, it was difficult for Duane to honestly ask God's blessing on the place and the people, but Claudia might remind him, interrupting the silence, "Come on, you know we don't got all night."

One slow late night at the Main Event, Claudia asked Duane for prayer—for herself. She told Duane that ever since her mother died in a fire, she had a weight on her heart. She didn't do enough, try hard enough, to save her mother from the fire. As Claudia explained the circumstances of the New Year's Eve fire that killed her mother and burned down the house, Duane realized he knew what she was describing. He was there. It was his first fire with the Akron Fire Department. He was able to tell her that there was nothing she could have done to save her mother.

He got better at bar ministry as time went on. Whatever discomfort he had experienced was gone as he saw the bar as a place that provided comfort and acceptance for people with no questions asked.

One Sunday, the Main Event hosted a fundraiser to support Duane's ministry.

After the bar closed the night of the fundraiser, a sewer line broke under Crosier Street. It undermined and structurally ruptured the length of the south basement wall of the bar. The Main Event never reopened. It was torn down. Today, the only evidence of its existence are the scars on the brick wall it shared with Old Glory Days, a strip club.

That a fundraiser for the ministry was the last event in a corner bar on South Main Street is a story that could never happen at South Street Ministries today, would not be on the planning flipchart paper at StratOps, but it had everything to do with the ministry's chemistry and genetics.

In 2017, though Duane was more often cruising the neighborhood in his car, he never bypassed the opportunity to connect with friends and strangers. His years as an EMS driver and a paramedic endowed his driving with a fluid character, just inside the edge of lawful behavior. His yardstick when they moved into Summit Lake was an inventory of public places of connection. Other than the corner stores and drive-thrus, there were fourteen bars and fourteen churches.

In 2017, the Main Event was not the only corner bar that had become a grassy open space. In fact, all the regular bars were gone. The two bars still existing on Main Street were strip clubs.

The other element of Duane's barometer was unchanged—there were still fourteen places of worship: twelve Christian churches, an Islamic

mosque, and a Buddhist temple. Duane's aim had been to bring the church
pew and the bar stool closer. Twenty years later, it seemed the barstools
were gone. Duane, appreciating the humor and the pathos of such a thing,
would also point out that many of the church pews tended to be dusty from
lack of use.

Some of the bars had become places of worship. Duane's own ministry,
South Street, found its home in what had been The Beer Garden. Ted's Bar,
the popular neighborhood place, became Peter Maurin Center, a soup
kitchen and shelter operated by the Akron Catholic Worker.

Just past the Peter Maurin Center, at the corner of Miller Avenue, South
Main smacks directly into the curve of the rail bed. This location is the
southeast corner edge of the fifty-eight-block Summit Lake neighborhood.
Here the road splits in two, with the left called South Main and the right
Old South Main. Nearly all vehicular traffic takes the left fork. It bridges
over the tracks at a pleasant angle and becomes a comprehensible two-way
street as it enters Firestone Rubber territory.

The right fork is an entry to the twilight zone. Old South Main curves
to the west, paralleling the railroad tracks. The curve introduces a kind of
forced perspective. In its compressive arc, the view exposes stationary freight
cars sitting on tracks. A weedy hill behind them is topped with the looming
power of the Firestone plant. In the absence of vehicular traffic on the wide
road, the scale and age of the buildings holding the curve add to the disori-
enting cultural nostalgia. It all shimmers on the threshold of the hallucina-
tory. For a second the sounds, smell, and feel of Akron's industrial muscle
are available to the open mind.

The tangible detritus of the fleeting cultural past remains intact inside
the triangular brick two-story building in the center of the curve. "Parasson's
Barbeque Restaurant" is faintly visible in peeling painted letters above the
six uniform boarded-up storefronts.

On Friday, March 4, four men associated with South Street were inside
the Parasson's building with flashlights, picking their way carefully through
the debris. This building was one of many the City of Akron wanted out of
its inventory. South Street Ministries was interested in its potential as a
neighborhood hub. The tour thus far was discouraging. The four men had
already inspected the basement and ground floor stores without Duane.

He was late, but in their experience with him, they knew he might be diverted by a spontaneous need. He had been depressed lately. But he would, as he always did, show up. The second floor did not alter their negative impression. When Duane bounded up the stairs to join them, he sparked, he was back to the guy who saw opportunities in the worst thing.

The second floor was a time capsule. A maze of doors topped with transoms opening to vignettes of life interrupted, it was a messy tribute to a male single occupancy hotel. A perfect distillation of sudden mysterious abandonment, it had the compelling quality of Chernobyl photographs. Renovation would seem to be beyond anyone's powers, but Duane saw it alive. He pointed out the great views and imagined artists living there, with local small businesses below, in the open commercial storefront spaces.

Duane asked the guys if it was ok that they pray together. Most of the men were accustomed to such a request. Among them was the grandson of Dallas Billington, founder of one of the country's first megachurches, the Akron Baptist Temple. When there was no objection, he asked Eric Harmon to lead them. They removed their caps. Fred Wheat, from City Planning, did the same, standing with the five others in a loose circle in the dingy hallway. Eric offered a general all-purpose sort of prayer followed by a minute of silence. What each of the six could have been praying for remained in their hearts. For Fred Wheat, in all his years of giving such tours, this was a first. He found it refreshing.

Duane inspires others to take up the vision for the future, but his fundamental calling is to the present. He looked around the place and saw the potential. He wasn't thinking about past disappointments, old efforts to change Old South Main. He wasn't weighed down by the memories around the neighborhood crusade to transform the BancOne annex building, one block away from where they stood. The city had their ideas, the neighborhood had theirs, and neither vision came to be.

The city eventually leased the BancOne site as a parking lot for the new Save-A-Lot. That a grocery store had opened in the neighborhood was a sign of change for the better.

Whether his ministry and the local triumph of churches over bars bears any relation to the drop in violent crime in Summit Lake is a matter of speculation. The reduction in crime corresponds to a reduction in population. The reduction in population resulted from unnatural forces: the crack epidemic, the housing mortgage crisis, and the policies of Mayor Don Plusquellic's administration.

The neighborhood is a safer, quieter place than it was twenty years ago. The racial breakdown is close to fifty-fifty, as it has been for decades. Today Asians and Hispanics account for about ten percent of the diminishing total. Kids still play in the streets, and there are more gardens and trees, fewer houses. Duane's consistent motivating energy is to do what Jesus would do. He lived the CCDA's three basic principles of reconciliation, relocation, and redistribution.[10]

"I call him Pastor now," says Miss Shirley Finney, the neighborhood connector, lifetime resident, and matriarch of Summit Lake. "He was one thing when he came, thinking he could save us all. We didn't need saving. But he stayed, he changed. He empowers others, steps aside but stays alongside. I call him pastor now."

Prayer is not measurable; grace cannot be weighed. In 2000, after two Palestinian store owners were killed within six months during robberies, Duane organized a mixed group of neighborhood men in prayer vigils to end the violence and calm the racial tension. There were no more shootings, no more store owners wounded or killed.

A more measurable point would be the number of times over those years that Duane and Lisa hosted friends on their living room couch for months, guys who became extra uncles for the Crabbs kids. There is a number for how many times did one of the kids shooting hoops in their front yard called out "Mr. Crabbs, watch this!" There could be an inventory of the bicycles repaired by kids over the twenty years of Bike Shop. Countable are the number of five-year-olds he lifted over his head and tossed up in the air. Countable too, are the number of people who walked away for good, and those who came back, and back again. For twenty years, this was the fidelity of Duane and Lisa. They were available.

By the spring of 2017 there were at least a dozen new "Duane 'n' Lisas" in the neighborhood, taking up the call to incarnational Christian practice that has become more identifiable as a movement. This next generation of "New Monastic" Christians has more to offer their concerned loved ones than the simple urging in Mark 10:21—"Come, take up the cross, and follow me." There are shelves of books that detail what Duane and Lisa have lived.

Among the practitioner writers is Shane Claiborne, the founder of The Simple Way. A charismatic southerner of prodigious energy and imagination, he has been a tremendous influence in the movement. His greatest contribution may be a mojo long absent from white Christianity—he is *cool*.

Terri Johnson, an Akron businesswoman inspired by Shane Claiborne, was looking for a way she could follow his example. More than one person said "Duane Crabbs." After some time in worship with South Street, she purchased a house in Summit Lake to allow others the incarnational experience. She committed to providing the shelter for those doing what she, in her full-time career, could not.

Stephanie Leonardi ("Leo") left her job as an art teacher in the Akron Public School system to live in the house Terri bought. Leo was the first resident of what came to be identified by the kids as Leo's House. She wanted to get to know the neighborhood before doing much of anything, trusting that cashing out her teacher's pension would last long enough until she did. Soon after Terri and a group of South Street regulars repainted the second floor, Patrick and Maggie, a freshly married couple intent on a missional life took the third floor. Whatever doubts neighbors on Long Street had about the churchy types moving in didn't last long. Leo had brought her trampoline with her.

With Duane and Lisa to check in with, Leo figured it out as she went along. She had a willingness to enter fully into the lives of her neighbors. As she cruised along on her motorbike or truck, choruses of kids shouted out her name. Creating participatory projects as neighborhood events, she brought hope and visibility to the participants and to the neighborhood. She had the spontaneous spirit that matched the lives of people in poverty and drove others crazy. She was fun, and like Duane, made people around her feel special.

The ideals of living in community are tested by living in community. The Long Street House residents shared similar values, but the dirty dish reality—the neighborhood visitors ringing the bell at any hour and kids on the trampoline—were points of friction for deeper divisions among the young Christian adults in the house.

In March of 2017, Leo accepted that the environment she envisioned was not where the household wanted to go. Despite being the first one in, her dreams did not carry more weight than the other four women in the house. She wanted to deepen her commitment to the people she loved, to the neighborhood. She started looking for her own house.

She saw one for sale closer to the lake and asked Dave Baker to take a look. Dave has a construction business and is a wizard of engineering. One of the very first people to support Duane and Lisa's vision, Dave had bought and personally renovated their house as a gift. He met Leo in the driveway before going in to check the building.

It had been twenty years since he stood with the Crabbs family in the driveway of 130 West South Street. Back then, in the pause before the first look inside the condemned house, they stopped, calming the nerves and excitement with prayer. Time and again over the two decades, Dave showed up with his ingenious energy to get any job done for friends at South Street. Leo and Dave stood together and prayed aloud in the driveway before they entered the house. It did not take long for him to recognize that it was a gem.

"It's a very good house," Dave Baker whispered during the survey.

The basement was plain vanilla, functional, and exposed. It was dry, odor free, with only a slight moisture in the masonry at the corners. In one corner was the typical feature of Akron houses of this era—the rubber worker's shower, first stop after a grimy shift at Firestone. The floor joists were full-dimension timber 2' x 8'. The electrics and plumbing were up to date. Everything was accessible, the copper lines running straight and true. The rest of the house was equally cared for. There was one minor leak over the rear entry door, an easy fix. The original woodwork was in splendid shape, in a pleasing diluted Craftsman style. From the second-floor windows, you could see Summit Lake.

"It's a very, very, good house," Dave pronounced, back in the sunny bite of March wind sweeping up from Summit Lake. Dave was happy, he looked great and was very much himself as he gave his clear generous assessment to Leo. You would not know that he was seriously ill with cancer. He had been given a window of how much time he could expect to live, and he was a man who would live fully to the very last breath. As he climbed back into his pickup truck, he announced that he was three days away from his eightieth birthday. "March fourth!" he called out, waving a fist in the air. In his workingman clothes in front of his truck, he looked like he could, at any minute, perform one of his legendary climbs up to the roof to fix that one spot that needed attention.

Fortunately with Leo's house, Dave's involvement didn't need to go further than the driveway diagnosis. He got in his truck, and with a wave and a thumbs-up he was off, back home to make lunch for his wife Marlene. She was also ill. Dave was determined to outlive her because he was afraid. Not over his approaching death, but his fears for her. Who would care for her after he died? He could not bear the idea of his Marlene facing life alone in declining health after sixty years of marriage together.

Duane and Lisa's decision to move to the neighborhood and the condition of the house they chose were staggeringly challenging to the status quo. Three years passed from the time Duane had brought the idea to the family. Lisa could not explain it, but one day she just knew.

"My heart just opened to the idea." Whatever doubts she had at the time stayed in her heart. Their decision prompted hostility from church friends. Family told them they were putting their children at risk for the sake of their idea of following Jesus. They were misunderstood, marginalized, and criticized, but they were committed to the courageous decision as partners. Though the decision to move to the neighborhood got the attention, most of the media coverage was a misrepresentation of the truth. The decision came of two people working out differences in the mutual bond of fidelity. Duane and Lisa chose obedience over comfort.

Twenty years later, Lisa realized that her greatest fear turned out to be her greatest gift. Her fear was for her children. Today, by any measure they are exemplary young adults. All four are working in service. Three out of the four live in Akron. As Lisa continues to do "some admin work" for South Street Ministries from home, she has a new companion in the living room. Three days a week she cares of their first grandchild, Elliott, born on Thanksgiving weekend, 2016.

By contrast, Leo's decision to move forward on home ownership in Summit Lake was a far simpler proposition by 2017. For Stephanie considering the commitment to the $25,000 house, there would still be some people who might think such a purchase dangerous and foolhardy. But not everyone. Neckties were turning in the direction of the charismatic body of water a hundred yards from her future front door.

Summit Lake was hot.

Not hot in the sense it had once been, actually hot; so hot with chemicals and waste heat from the Firestone Pump House that it would not freeze in winter. No, it was civic and real estate hot. White people were kayaking in it. The Ohio Fish and Game Commission declared the fish in it were safe to eat. That kind of hot.

Twenty years before, Summit Lake wore a shroud of physical and psychic dimension. The last full environmental analysis of the lake was done in 1978. The three-second view while passing on the interstate was lovely, but it was otherwise all but invisible as a resource. The foliage and weeds around the lake were so thick at the edges, it was invisible to those living on the eastern side of the lake. The weeds were too high to see the water.

Snap

Donovan Harris was not surprised easily. His background, intelligence, and personality equipped him with a capacity to see the whole board. It's a point of pride that he knew what was coming without seeing it. He had the sense of the moves to come. But Duane was a complete surprise, starting from the day they finally met.

Before they met, Donovan had been to the café a few times, "the brick place on Grant, the one with that fire red roof." He was tuned to qualities most people don't notice. He came into a new situation and listened for subtleties below the range of ears alone. It was more of the rhythm, sound, and energy all in one. It was the pulse of a place he could feel through his skin. Akron had it, definitely. Front Porch Café had it, had its own pulse. He had a good feeling in there.

Eric and Joe told him he had to meet their pastor. From the way they talked about him, Donovan assumed Duane was Black. So the surprise of meeting a white guy further rattled the unsettling vague emotions. Donovan had just passed the point of being out of prison longer than he had been in. At forty-three, he knew he was coming into a new phase of his life but struggled not to come into it blindsided.

A neutral stance in new situations came through decades of navigating the continuously new. Donovan had learned not to judge, not to rule out any potential avenues for a possibility he might not be able to name but at least keep in his pocket. Growing into manhood incarcerated, he knew any expectation or assumptions could be dangerous.

"I met all kinds in prison. Friendships are formed on a different set of standards."

One of his trusted mates inside was the head of the Aryan Nation, a guy who had been in for forty-five years.

"I had a wide group of trusted friends, including gay guys. Like most straight men, I assumed that all gays wanted me, just because I was a man. But I found out it works the same way as straight. Attraction is specific, not universal."

He came to the meeting with Duane in another new personal situation, something that made him jittery and insecure. And though his experience told him that he could figure a way through such things, he was still scared where he stood, nervous in this unusual specific.

In March 2014, John Lucas' documentary film *Cooler Bandits* opened at the Cleveland International Film Festival. The power of the documentary brought a new kind of attention. Notoriety was not new to Donovan Harris, but the publicity around the movie brought a kind of celebrity to Donovan and his friends that was familiar but not. They were on stage again, feeling defined again by something they could not control. After putting fourteen years in making a life on the outside, his identity was at stake from a new version of his past.

Donovan described himself and his friend Frankie as just bored high school kids looking and playing "gangsta" while hanging around Chapel Hill Mall. Both sharp and smart, they challenged each other, scheming plans around getting money without dealing drugs. Though they both had minimum wage service jobs, they were talking about real money.

Frankie's experience at Kentucky Fried Chicken was the basis of the bored afternoon scheme. He often opened or closed the restaurant and had the routine down. The transition time was quiet. There were no customers and few employees. With so few people around, they could do the robbery without anyone getting hurt. It was a plan that could really work. Excited by the potential for the crime, they planned the rest of the details carefully.

Their plan succeeded. Armed with Ninja turtle masks, a toy gun, and a getaway car, the teenage robbers had instant money. By ushering the employees into the walk-in cooler, they had sufficient time to get away without anyone getting hurt. Donovan, the youngest of the gang of three, made the call to 911 after they fled the scene. As much as they worked out the operation, they had not planned beyond the initial success. They had what they wanted, easy money. It worked. And it worked again. Their formula became a franchise.

They kept going to high school. No one suspected they were the men behind the string of armed robberies. The toy became a real gun over the course of their heists. One time the staff was locked in the freezer. Over the twelve-month crime spree, they acquired an identity in the *Akron Beacon Journal*. They had a name. They were the "The Cooler Bandits."

The *Beacon* extensively followed the drama of the capture and subsequent trials of the four main robbers, though during the trials they never published photos of the defendants. There was no doubt that they had committed the twelve robberies they were accused of; the issue was more about sentencing. The suffering of the victims was traumatic, though none were physically hurt.

Donovan had turned himself in and hired his own lawyer. He went for a plea bargain and received the shortest sentence, sixteen to twenty years. Frankie Porter, defiant and uncooperative during the trial, was found guilty of all counts against him, got a combined sentence of five hundred years.

Fortunately for the other three, Donovan, Charlie Kelly, and Richard Roderick, they served their time in the same facility, the majority at Mansfield Correctional Facility. After fourteen years, the last nine at Mansfield Correctional Facility, Donovan was the first of the four to be released. He came back to Akron, his home and place he loved, opened his own office-cleaning business, and grew into the dad he dreamed about for his own two children.

But after fourteen years of steady growth, the release of the documentary stirred up an uncomfortable foreign anxiety. Donovan wanted nothing to do with the attention generated around the movie, the story, or the version of himself people took from the movie. He was thinking about his two children, trying to steer through the unwanted attention while not denying his past and his sense of obligation to give back.

Donovan did his best thinking at night, alone, while cleaning a client's offices. The rhythm and routine of making things new, whether cleaning the toilets or against the backdrop of the steady hum of the vacuum cleaner, the pendulum swing of the floor polisher. It was a familiar and safe neutrality for working things out. The friendship with Duane was forged in a similar crucible. He felt at ease with Duane's feathered assurance behind the wheel as they cruised through the city they loved, side by side, facing the same direction.

As they got familiar, Donovan was struggling to maintain his North Hill Main Street drop-in center, Gravity. Aside from some sputtering youth programs in the storefront, the activity was confined to the back office, the only room with heat. Even so, the men in the weekly accountability group kept their coats on and clutched their coffee cups. Duane became a regular in the group.

After one of the meetings, Donovan and Duane walked down the block to check out a new ministry. The two men liked being in motion together. The streets and sidewalks of Akron suited their rhythm. It was an Akron thing, the snap, the pop, the love of the ground of it, standing on the sidewalk, hands in pockets, having the time and taking the time to make a space together for what comes along. The ministry was closed, but its bold contemporary Christian branding blared its way across the plate glass. "Bridging the Gap" took over a building Donovan remembered fondly from his childhood as Lentine's Music Shop. He and his friends were welcomed in the store to play the instruments. It was a special place in the neighborhood without a lot of alternatives.

As they walked back to Gravity, Duane described "Bridging the Gap" as another helicopter ministry for the poor, another set of people from outside with assumptions, dropping off salvation and flying off. He said the place would better serve the neighborhood if it was still a music store.

Whoa. As they got closer to Gravity, Donovan realized he was another variation on storefront ministry. His building was more of a tribute to his ego than an instrument for change. His prayer groups and youth groups could be found in any of the old buildings strung along the commercial streets of North Hill. If he was sincere about real change, he needed to tear it up and start over.

After he gave up the lease, he started working from the corner round table at the Front Porch Café. His business card had a conventional business

address, something he freely admitted was still ego, but his real work happened at the table, on the day-to-day working of the café life. It just clicked
for him there.

Donovan started his corner office as Eric Harmon was on his way out
of the building he had managed for seven years. The renovation project was
finished, Eric completed his master's degree in divinity and was actively
looking for a position as a prison chaplain. In his final months at South
Street, he spent more time alone in the basement than upstairs. His desk
was covered with detritus and half-consumed lunches, with the only open
spot the zone of his laptop.

Few ventured down to find him. He could hear anyone well before they
got close, since getting to him involved descending an open wood stair,
crossing through a dark storage area and over a moat by means of a plank
of wood over an open gravel channel of a steady underwater stream remnant.

In June 2015, the offer from Mansfield Correctional Facility came the
same day as the Certificate of Occupancy for the Front Porch project. He
brushed off the debris from the basement desk. Eleven years before, he got
out of prison in Oklahoma. As a married man with two young daughters,
a new career, and a collar, he was going back inside.

~

After three years as the prison chaplain, Eric enjoyed the hour drive
from his gracious Queen Anne home in Highland Square to Mansfield.
Unlike South Street, where there was often no separation between the job
and home, working at the prison was completely separate from his private
life. The commute gave him time alone to think and pray. It was not as good
as fishing for working things out, but it was two solid hours every day
between the extremes of his home life with his wife and now three daughters and his work life with inmates and staff.

He had been working through a challenge on his commute. For three
years as chaplain, he had tried and learned different ways of walking alongside the men. Right from the start, the job was easier than he expected. He
met little resistance from the inmates or the administration for the way he
channeled a spiritual program. Though his practice was primarily Christian,
he often facilitated other religious traditions as needed. He loved his work.

Now he had a guy, a recent convert to Christianity, asking questions and showing curiosity about a new way of living. The inmate recently had ten years added to his sentence for operating as a gang leader inside Mansfield and was denied participation in the Bible study group. Eric thought the man was ready to lead a group of guys that might not otherwise come to a Bible study.

Eric thought bringing Duane and Donovan as guest speakers for a selected group of inmates could be a way to advance his idea. He invited them to Mansfield.

Donovan knew that Christianity in prison is viewed as the least and worst thing to be a part of. "It's for softies and stoolies. The snitches tell the pastor, and the pastor tells the authority."

But he also said that Christianity was what could make you free. "Islam, the popular prison faith, told you what to do, when to pray. It's regimented. Christianity is not at all regimented; it requires an inner strength. It's about strength. I found Christianity in prison when I was not looking for it."

It had been eighteen years since Donovan had been inside Mansfield Correctional. He walked out in 1998, after serving the last nine of his fourteen years of incarceration there. As he and Duane waited at security for their clearance, it was a change of shift. The staff called out to each other; their voices friendly but too loud in the bare room. The sound bounced around the concrete block walls, tile floor, and metal detectors. It was a harsh blur of sound. No one seemed to mind, they were used to it. Donovan felt the tightening.

Eric, a big smile above his clerical collar and ID pass, came in from the yard and waited on the other side as Donovan and Duane cleared the metal detector and were issued their passes. As they crossed the yard, Eric and Duane talked as Donovan's feet carried him into the past. The trees had grown. They were planted close to the end of his time, and the rumor was they would have cameras and guns in the branches.

The trees had grown, the doors to the pods were a different color, but everything else was the same, same, same. The sounds and smells, same. Donovan was a jumble of emotions, things going on, memory, pain, stuff he could not allow himself to feel as they sat down in a circle with the men. He was pushing away the panic of being inside.

What secured him, what made it alright that day was Duane. Duane was there with him, and his usual self—comfortable, relaxed, easy, and present. He had the attention so Donovan could just keep breathing. Looking at Duane helped him with the emotions, connected him to something other than the unexpected trip into the loop of prison.

He did not say anything to Duane. But through the terror of being back inside, he was able to get to the grief of growing up inside. Because everything was the same, there was no way to avoid it. While they were there, he was back in there. But seeing Duane gave him a rope, a way to grieve the time. Walking back the way they came in, he looked at the trees with relief.

He left the grief there. It was over. The suppressed pain had shifted, lifted. Snap. The trees had grown.

Margins

In early spring of 2016, buildings all along South Main and Broadway were reduced to pyramids of red brick, demolished in preparation for the reconfiguration of access roads to the Central Interchange. Leo wanted to take pictures before it was all gone. She rode around in her black pickup truck with the purple hubcaps, inviting Summit Lake kids to join in. Her young friends posed in front of the red rubble, and Leo took some pictures. No real reason, just because it was happening. Just because it was fun. Just because it was something to do. Just because it was Leo.

Months later, when asked to represent South Akron at the Big Love Festival, Leo thought of the pictures of kids and bricks. She enlarged one to 5' x 7' and hung it vertically along the back wall of her designated space on the third floor of the Summit Art Space. In front of the picture, she arranged a pile of loose bricks. That was all. No handouts or printed material. Just the picture and the bricks.

The South Akron stall had a great placement. It was right across from the entry door on the third floor. After walking up two flights of stairs, it was the first thing a visitor saw stepping into the open space. The picture had the power spot and made the most of it.

The photograph conveyed something that was instantly recognizable. It was real. The viewer and the kids met each other in the space between. It had a quality that reminded us that most of what we see is contrived. It was simply the world of those children at that moment. It directly conveyed a beauty, a kind of ordinary redemptive presence.

There was a joy and hope in it too. It was all there and made for the unforgettable surprise instant that art bestows on the unsuspecting viewer. There, in the still point of the margins of the marginalized, kids just being themselves. Her impulse to document the changes along the eastern boundary of the Summit Lake neighborhood captured something about the soul of the whole neighborhood. The picture showed a physical wrenching change in the jagged pile of bricks behind the children. But beyond that rough obvious physical change, there was so much latent change in the image. Things were certainly going to change, for the artist, Leo—and maybe, who knows, the kids in the picture and Summit Lake itself.

Leo had the personal qualities and creative energy to attract a curious crowd, and she invited the curious to join her. She was inspired by Duane, and he saw in Leo a version of himself. They both had a fire in their bones for the suffering of those around them, and they were not afraid to enter that suffering. Leo had a rare combination of the true believer and the freedom of a true artist. She saw her religious faith as the fuel for her expression of art. She saw the art as a means of connection.

For almost three years, Leo had been in the neighborhood without a job. The year before the move, she was a full-time art teacher in the Akron Public School system and barely survived a systemic septic infection. After her recovery from the brink of death, she was not the same teacher she had been. The work she loved seemed strange now, classroom walls too close. She suspected the school building itself had made her sick.

Through the slow physical, emotional, and spiritual recovery, she felt a continuing pull to grow with South Street's ministerial outreach in Summit Lake. Through the perplexing moments of navigating a blank road map, Duane and Lisa were close by and available. For Leo, they were parents, peers, friends, and coworkers. But they were at a different place in life, and for as much as they shared in the passion of living out the Word, she could feel lonely after leaving their company, riding alone in the black pickup with the purple hubcaps towards the home she shared with four other women.

Leo was starting to recognize she operated better without a framework. She was a disciplined improviser, mixing up what was available to invent something new. She made it look easy, fun, clean, complete, and exciting. There was an undeniable power and attraction to Leo that made everyone want to jump in first, ask later.

Her unadorned Mediterranean classic features were framed by baggy sports clothes. It wasn't calculated, her charm and beauty, rather it was the self-made personality of someone who had to make their own way emotionally at too early an age. There was a wildness in her, a Peter Pan quality. It was a quality that, while immensely attractive, could burn too fast with new friends deciding it was all more adventure than they really wanted after all.

A year later, in the spring of 2017, the Summit Lake neighborhood was clamped tight on its edges. Big money pressed against the margins of the old community. Civic projects of contrasting aspirational goals stirred up the east and west sides. The opposing compass points were expressive of the projects themselves, polar opposites, and a distorted mirror of the extremes of the human experience. The fifty-eight-block old neighborhood was the unwitting host of a fringe population, outsiders reshaping both flanks.

On the west, it was all about the highest aspirations, while the east addressed the lowliest necessity. Along the western edge, defined by the shoreline of Summit Lake, the money and attention were all about art; on the eastern side, defined by the active rail lines, it was all about better disposal of human effluent; as per mandate by the Environmental Protection Agency, work continued on getting Akron's literal shit out of the Cuyahoga River.

~

For a season in the grand American bazaar of the marketing of all things, the term *liminal space* whipped around the corridors of branding experts and then fell out of fashion. It was a trendy way of describing risk-takers, edge-walkers, marginalized populations, people, and things generally that did not fit. Overused, the term itself was then cast to the margins.

There was a lot of talk about liminal spaces. *Limnology* as a scientific pursuit is the study of edge communities, the unique qualities of environments that thrive at the meeting line of two distinct systems. In the spring of 2017 in Summit Lake, there was a liminal rhythm, a continuous wave of change from the edges that could not be tuned out. On the Eastern Front, for two years prior to the spring of 2017, the landscape of South Main and Broadway endured constant pummeling and shoving. The reconfiguration of ramps and access to the freeway, billed as a "new entrance to downtown Akron" had removed nearly all the remnants of a half-mile chunk of the commercial and industrial life and history of South Main and Broadway. All the trees on South Main were marked with a neon X one day, and not long after, surgically removed in the course of one night, consigned to mulch, not a chip, leaf, or twig left on the devil strip. The only indication of their existence the day before was a series of rhythmic shallow holes and a host of birds circling overhead.

In addition to the highway project, a new set of operators came to the scrubbed surface in the spring of 2017. This crew folded into the blanched landscape to install new massive sewage lines for the enthusiastically titled "Akron Waterways Renewed!" The work on Main and Broadway was one small link in an enormous and necessary project. It added to the already beleaguered bottleneck of local and commuter car traffic just trying to get from A to B.

The work brought a whole new set of unrecognizable manufactured items to the muddy landscape along the railroad tracks. The barren ground was dotted with a mysterious array of enormous concrete piping, complex gauges, and continuously humming machinery devoted to the new storm water sewage treatment system for the City of Akron.

Navigating that section by car became extremely challenging. Giant heaps of earth and earthmovers dominated and determined the flow of traffic. Running the gauntlet of orange cones outlining one lane of the reduced road along a sizable stretch of South Main Street was a steel-nerved, white-knuckle driving experience. The shape of the lane could change on a daily basis, as though the gods were playing chess with traffic cones. To make matters worse, the streetlights were gone. It had the eerie feeling of entering a funhouse, or approaching the edge of a cliff, or the end of the known world.

It became almost impossible to tell visitors how to get to the neighborhood. There simply was no way in without going downtown and doubling back.

How do you know when your neighborhood doesn't matter?
When you can't get to it.

~

Meanwhile, on the western side of the neighborhood, two organizations
arranged themselves around the scuffled shoreline of Summit Lake. With
the lofty goals of creating art and building community, representatives of
two distinct Knight Foundation grant initiatives called on the community
to join in the process. In contrast with the concrete reality of the work on
the opposite margin, the goals on the Summit Lake Shore had no defined
outcomes. "The League of Creative Interventionists" and "Reimagining
Civic Commons" shared a lot of similar qualities beyond their ambiguous
names. It all had something to do with pushing for a change in perceptions
about community, art, and local input. There was money behind the language
and marketing trying to draw in Summit Lake residents. The local population was suspicious of what they saw as municipal bait-and-switch operations,
of new language from the same old downtown carnival barkers. In meetings
at the Summit Lake Community Center, Dan Rice effused the potential of
the Knight-funded "Civic Commons" project before donning an apron to
serve dinner after the meetings, his enthusiasm unflagging despite the wary
distance of those who showed up.

"Why should we trust you?" Darrell called out from the back of the
room on one such night, hands deep in the pockets of his blue quilted jacket.

"We're going to try some things together," Dan said.

Rice, as the president of the Ohio & Erie Canalway Coalition for over
twenty-five years, had miles of experience in fielding public forums and the
stirred emotions that accompany change. "Everything we do will be with
you, what you want to see here on your lakefront. And it's all an experiment,
temporary—we will try things, and if it's not right, we will try something
else—but they will be your ideas, so spread the word to your neighbors.
This is your project."

Though the neighborhood is less than two miles from the benchmark
intersection of downtown, Market and Main Streets, it is confined and
isolated by its hard, defining edges: a lake, a freeway, and a rail line. The
attention at the edges was an intervention for a community aging steadily

in a kind of benign spiral of diminishing energy, the pulse slowing, the sag and fade of geography in hospice care. The work on both sides of the neighborhood was all about flow, and that energy vibrated the skin of the neighborhood. The outside attention was met with skepticism in front porch conversations; it was all a part of the master plan to create a new Summit Lake that did not include them.

Both undertakings aim at a better future for the Greater Akron community. Both constitute a level of attention and interest around an area slowly drifting downward for decades without much attention from the previous city administration.

This neighborhood wears the weight of failed hopes and present pain. Having a dream of something different is not free; it comes at the cost of more disappointment. This was a place grown so accustomed to neglect, the barometer for what services should be expected in a neighborhood was broken. Cars parked with impunity on the sidewalk in front of the Xclusive Gentlemen's Club on South Main, active construction zones lacked protective fencing, and trying to walk across the broad area of highway and sewer work on the east side was dangerous and discouraging. All the grade crossings of the rail line were eliminated in the expressway project, requiring a pedestrian to walk an extra half-mile at least, along disjointed spaces right next to car traffic. The cars frightened the people walking and the walking people frightened the drivers of the cars.

Ironically, though the neighborhood was cut off from the city surrounding it, Summit Lake has express connections with the world beyond the city. Access to the freeway system allows vehicles a quick hit, in and out of the neighborhood from and to all four directions. This drive-thru capacity had disastrous consequences when crack hit the Midwest in the late eighties. Summit Lake was old and modest at the beginning of the crack epidemic, but stable. It had no defense against its geography and the tide of cheap, available drugs flowing in and out. By the start of the nineties, the neighborhood had the second highest crime rate in Akron.

In the Summit Lake neighborhood, the largest active organization, since the closing of Lincoln Elementary School, bigger than any commercial enterprise or church in the neighborhood, is a faith-based service provider, the Open M neighborhood center. This ministry offers a variety of services for a neighborhood steadily depopulating. The neighborhood suffered not from a lack of free giveaways. It suffered from too many give-aways and too few people.

~

The bread and butter of South Street's light-touch evangelism are com-munity meetings. So it was not unusual for Joe Tucker and Leo to attend those meetings advancing the Knight-funded art projects. They joined in with the sparse group of local activists willing to give time to listen to yet another set of presenters with ideas for the neighborhood.

Duane had been one of the founders of the organization hosting the meetings, the Summit Lake Neighborhood Association. Other attendees that spring were mostly long-term resident activists, suspicious and accus-tomed to variations on this routine many times before. Recreational super-visor Audley McGill, with over thirty years of history at the Summit Lake Community Center, is polite while walking through the pattern. The trail of past failed promises was on the table along with the pizza. The format was familiar—enthusiastic smiling, suited white men with a PowerPoint presentation, markers, and whiteboard.

For the residents who came to the meetings, it was hard at first to understand who was who in the mix of these outsiders talking about art. It all sounded polished and it looked snazzy. But it was hard to keep things straight between the two Knight funded initiatives. The names of the organizations alone—The League of Creative Interventionists and Reimag-ining Civic Commons—were hard to retain.

Community-created art and placemaking are not new, but they were new to Summit Lake. Both the organizations, vying for the attention of local participation, spoke in the language of experimentation, of testing out ideas. Both were based outside Akron, and both clamored for space and attention. They both needed local buy-in for the success of the public art projects. They needed a trusted local to encourage the rest of the neighbor-hood to come along, to address the doubt. They needed an artist.

Leo knew something about public art. She made it all the time. Leo was fully engaged in the lives of the neighborhood kids. She was bringing children into stuff that she had always loved doing as a kid—sports and making art.

This was instinctive for her. She was a natural. It was easy to spot her bright pictographic style over the boarded-up windows of the second floor of the Front Porch Café and popping up in other places in town.

In the summer before the outside grant projects parked on Summit Lake, Leo imagined a big colorful mural in the intersection of Edison and West Long. It was a tricky corner, a three-way stop with four streets. It was part of a public bus route. Diagonally across the street from each other were two attractions for local children—the Let's Grow Akron Children's garden and the playground of Miller Church. Leo saw the mural as a community crosswalk, as a way to mix safety and art.

Her method of engaging the public was to sit at the picnic table on the grounds of Miller Avenue Church every Saturday through the summer of 2016. She laid out a big black-and-white plan of the intersection with heaps of crayons and markers for people to dream up ideas for the mural.

Some of the target participants came over after the regular Saturday lunch inside the church. If they had not eaten their lunch inside, Leo asked them over to eat and chat. She called out to whoever passed by to come over and sketch, to bring home small copies of the site plan. She knew almost everybody by name. Not everyone was interested or knew what she was talking about, but most everyone liked hanging out with Leo.

The painting of the mural party was open to all. The day began at sunrise, blocking all the streets and blasting the intersection with the power washer. It was a Sunday. Duane called the painting party to be the church service for the day. Within the familiar outline of a block party, there was the totally unfamiliar imperative to transfer the final design to the intersection, one thousand square feet of eight different colors blooming in five-gallon buckets.

Throughout the day, there was music, food, and side games, punctuated by the joyful shrieks of children running through a lawn sprinkler. The Akron rock stacker added a meditative touch back from the center of the action. A basketball hoop stayed busy on another arm of the blocked intersection.

By six o'clock, it was done. Everyone who had participated signed the work on the corner where the street met the curb cut. A drone that had been buzzing around most of the day took the group photo, a tight happy bunch around the signatures. Something had been made that was owned by the whole group. The signatures were there, ownership proved by inclusion in the happy tag.

So where art was concerned, if Leo bought into the merits of these foreign dream-spinners, others would follow. She was unsure herself, at first, of the intentions of the new arrivals. They were operating out of a payroll and a program. Their work came from a motivation that was different, but she was willing to hope, to join in.

～

On its own merits, the Summit Lake neighborhood has an organic beauty, a graceful air. There is a patina of age in the craftsmanship of hundred-year-old houses that alternate with the empty lots. Proportion, scale, and detailing in the porches and size of the houses bespeak of an era of larger families and summer heat endured by staying in the shade of the front porch. Abundant still, that grace, if through a filter of broken bicycles, odd household and industrial debris, and clumsy wooden wheelchair ramps snaking over a once broad set of entry steps.

That grace is still abundant in the walk of Shirley Finney, with a lifetime in the neighborhood. She moves with a tempo between poem and prayer, feet grounded in the place, head tilted at an angle that arcs the spirit of Summit Lake. She has not forgotten how it was and how it got to be what it is now. But she stays in it, in the hospitality and observation from her front porch, not in the filter of the broken debris. It's the steel resolve to reality with the melody that harkens to something else about what life was when everyone knew each other, for generations of knowing. In her song, Summit Lake is, as it has always been, a lady. Miss Finney's lady cut in two, but still, a lady. That too, is the essence of it, art. We know it when we see it, though we cannot name it.

But prior to 2014, there was nothing that anyone would describe as deliberate public art. Beyond street markers and stop signs, there were the modest and basic signage for the corner stores and bars. Any graphic marketing artistry was directed to the cars passing by, in the form of illuminated billboards high in the air. The neighborhood, with a slow pedestrian view, got the view of the giant foot for such messages, bolted on concrete in weedy empty parking lots.

Graphics and color at the eye level of residents tended to be in motion, on the sides of buses. The Akron Transit Bus Garage is on one edge of the neighborhood, in what had once been the streetcar barn. There is a steady parade of homeward bound buses at certain times of day, telegraphing color and code. NEED A LAWYER? or INJURED?! accompany larger than life pictures of wheelchair-bound victims. Huge tags and multi-color graffiti adorn the sides of containers rolling through the neighborhood, on freight trains not stopping in Akron.

Along with the question "What is public art?" there is the question that follows—"Who gets to make the art?"

And who gets to make the decision about who makes the art? Are artists from bigger places with more commissions and experience a better choice than a local artist?

With the engineering work involved in the transformation of the west side, no one would challenge the wisdom of outside consultants being hired. It was a massive coordination effort, in addition to the work itself. Two such infrastructure projects intersected along Old Main Street. Prior work for the new configuration of ramps and access to the highway, billed as a "new entrance to Downtown Akron" had removed nearly all the remnants of the commercial history of South Main and Broadway. The new sewer work exposed the old brick lined manholes as the new massive concrete pipes were installed for "Akron Waterways Renewed!"

That outside consultants would be hired for making the new sewer project is not a matter for debate. The main feature of "Akron Waterways Renewed!" is the creation of a one-mile-long tunnel, thirty feet in diameter, running diagonally under downtown Akron. Not many people are capable of creating a gigantic tunnel under a working city.

But when it comes to matters more subtle than engineering, then what? When questions of expertise are outside of measurable standards, what is the criteria for decision making? Who is the expert about the unquantifiable, who sets the standard for neighborhood beauty and meaning?

Real art can be scary because it reaches inside in a way that is unexpected. It shakes us up. That is the whole point. So rather than actual art, most publicly funded works tend to be more palatable than challenging. There is nothing wrong with this, but it ain't art. The current mission statement of the National Endowment for the Arts reads: "The National Endowment for the Arts is an independent federal agency that funds, promotes, and strengthens the creative capacity of our communities by providing all Americans with diverse opportunities for arts participation."[11]

This mission statement has led to work that seeks to engage communities, ushering in our current cultural preference for comfort over provocation.

Ironically the safer impulse trended towards communist ideals of "people's art." The goal dovetails with efforts to renovate abandoned urban spaces. The new mission statement has led to the creation of a new field for renewal of derelict public space: placemaking. The word, the idea, the concept has become an international movement, a college degree.

It hit the shore of Summit Lake in the spring of 2017.

The two Summit Lake grant projects operated out of the placemaking mindset. The artists from Seattle with the impossible name, The League of Creative Interventionists (The League) specialize in "events creation" such as elaborately orchestrated community meals and installations in neglected spaces. These gatherings photograph very well and live after their theatrical moment in the websites of the artists and foundations. Participants leave with a souvenir of the event that they helped to create. The events are momentary groundings in community, a reminder of other possibilities, in a place that for whatever reason, had become stale, taken for granted or simply unseen altogether.

The other group, with the equally difficult to remember name (Reimagining the Civic Commons) tried out ideas with a sense of fun: a giant foam marble rolling in downtown Akron and loose folding beach chairs on Main Street.

~

As the discussions about placemaking and public art started up at the community center, just beyond the immediate neighborhood there is a quintessential piece of public art from another era. It was a powerful symbol of what it represented, which was complete domination over the day-to-day lives of the people living in Summit Lake.

This bit of public art lives quietly beyond the giant red neon sign etched against the sky, visible day and night above Firestone's Plant 1, with the single word F I R E S T O N E. The illuminated word is an iconic entity, a beacon of the past. It is a landmark and a benchmark for orientation in South Akron, but really, it is not selling anything other than a cultural connection to memory.

Every night without fail, it lights up the skyline of South Akron. But it has been forty years since the last commercial tire came off the assembly line. The sign is a beacon almost entirely devoid of content. The building it rises above is nearly empty, its front door handles connected by spider webs. One type of high-end racing tire is produced within the enormous city-owned building. The sign conveys a message that is disjointed from reality. The sign is art.

The former manufacturing grounds of the Firestone campus are off-limits to the public, but one can wander in the open, modern areas of the campus to the south of the sign and find the bronzed figure of Harvey Firestone himself, gazing over this sign and the entirety of his former empire. Restored and ignored, the statue is devoid of contemporary connection, compelling, mysterious, and strange.

By the summer of 2017, the neighborhood that had served up the labor for the factory, would again come into a strange communion with its former boss. Despite the size of the Bridgestone/Firestone campus today, the living memory of its dominance is slight in the neighborhood now. Older residents are few. Shirley, eighty-five, lives in the house she grew up in on Paris Street. She worked at the Firestone bank at the corner of Miller and South Main for over thirty years. Her deceased husband was a painter at the plant.

"Not the regular kind of painting. He went up and down—elevator shafts. Now and then, Chuck would repaint F I R E S T O N E on the side of the smokestacks. That was Chuck's job."

But, from the perspective of art, urban archeology, and history, the neighborhood and the factory still have a lot of karma to work out. In the summer of 2017, it would manifest in a strange way. It rose through questions of legitimacy: Why are artists from outside Akron being given money and opportunity to make art about Akron? That question linked the community art process in the neighborhood with the statue gazing in frozen perpetuity at the evolving life of Summit Lake.

~

While all the Akron rubber companies prospered from defense work in World War II, the postwar era gave Firestone Tire and Rubber Company an additional reason to celebrate. Five years after Allied forces declared victory, the company would mark fifty years since its founding by founder Harvey Samuel Firestone. His five sons had plenty of cash to properly commemorate the monumental success of their father and his company. For a suitable memorial to the self-made titan, they could afford to hire the best money could buy.

This was a private, corporate decision, but with an overriding concern for public perception. There was no public agency with a voice in the process, but the sons intended to create a work for the public and for the expanding horizon of Firestone's future prosperity. The unveiling of the commissioned statue was scheduled as part of the fiftieth anniversary of the company. The half-century mark celebration included indoor and outdoor exhibitions, picnics, international visitors, and two circuses.

The three men commissioned for creating the memorial were famous and well respected. The designer was a New York architect, Eric Gugler. Franklin Delano Roosevelt had hired him to redesign the West Wing of the White house. He in turn recommended James Earle Fraser for the statue and Donald DeLue for additional stone sculptures completing the memorial ensemble. They worked in the classical repertoire associated with the refinement of the Greek and Roman revival style common to Washington, DC, and filtered through every state and town's design for evocation of authority and legitimacy.

The *Beacon Journal* predicted it would "give Akron a new center of cultural beauty." The statue of Firestone would be the crown, the centerpiece of the memorial assembly and of the twenty-five-acre campus sloping downward from the memorial monument.

This is placemaking along the lines of Louis XIV, the Sun King. All of South Akron and the Firestone factory lie below the circular design of the monument. By the time of the event on August 3, 1950, the attention on the unveiling was high. Firestone executives from ten countries, local dignitaries, religious leaders, *Life Magazine*, employees, and the curious all gathered as the five sons of the founder stood below the veiled gray bulk, sitting on a solid granite plinth, ten thousand necks craning upward. Before the multitude, the Metropolitan Opera soprano Eleanor Steber led the Firestone chorus in "Oh God Our Hope in Ages Past, Our Hope for Years to Come" as the five Firestone brothers pulled the cord to reveal the statue for the first time.

Memorials telegraph the values of the moment they are created more so than the subject memorialized. There were changes in the tire industry at that very moment signaling the end of Akron's dominance in keeping the world on the move. Harvey Firestone, gazing benignly from the armchair at his mile of empire in South Akron, was looking at the past, not the future.

Seeing the memorial today, it is as its architect Eric Gugler boasted at the dedication, "the elements composing it are of rare beauty and dignity." The original scotch pines have been replaced by three thornless honey locust trees, which have grown protectively around the assembly. A contemporary carpet of alternating grass and concrete squares connect it to the Bridgestone Research Building, completed in 2012. But the current attempt to connect it to its setting, which also includes handsome new but uninviting black stone benches, only increases its message of distance. It feels set apart, lonely, detached, and uncomfortably graceful.

The gaze of the titan has enough ambiguity to suit a range of interpretations. His left foot extends over the granite plinth, as though to launch him into a new big idea. It is possible to reach up an arm and touch the foot of the man who stomped over the landscape. But unlike Arnolfo di Cambio's *St. Peter Enthroned* in the Basilica of St. Peter in Rome, there is no sign of wear at Harvey's toe, the one point of connection. The urge to touch is dampened by some kind of hesitancy, the feeling of being watched. He is frozen in an idealized state, the veneer of what the culture wanted to believe about painless progress.

American culture is still in thrall of the self-made man, the bootstrap success stories, but we also want the backstories that characterize most of us. American culture wants and needs the stories around the base of the statue, those below the toe of the Caucasian male Christian foot.

In the summer of 2017, the need for embracing more, all of the truth of the American story became frighteningly clear. It became clear through

a dramatic shift in perception around public art. If most white Americans
didn't think much about the bronze representations of Confederate military
in the public spaces of cities and towns throughout the South, it became
impossible not to recognize that the statues held different messages for
Black Americans. These were statues honoring men who were defending
the right of some people to own other people. Art became a passionate
focus for reexamining who we are and who we aspire to be.[12] That the statues
had to go was clear. But the opportunity for a broader discussion about
culture, about our shared public spaces, did not happen. In the intense
discomfort, escalating to fear and violence,[13] most of the statues were removed
at night, as quickly as a ton of bronze on a ten-foot granite base can be taken
out of sight.

Though Harvey's bronze likeness is dressed in period clothing, he has
just cast off a classical robe of some sort, perhaps indicating his personal
rejection of the elevated status he so obviously deserves. Perhaps the discarded robe is meant to signal his identification with the common man,
with his workers, with the world extending beyond the reach of Firestone
Rubber.

Bronze Harvey watched the steady diminishment of his creation. In
2012, his view of the empire he built was obscured by the construction of
the Bridgestone Americas Technical Center. Firestone exists today as one
part of a Japanese corporation with its headquarters in Tokyo, Japan.

In the summer of 2017, however, a new artistic movement had grown
around the far edge of his former empire. Beyond the lowest point of his
ambiguous gaze, on the shore of Summit Lake, the former Firestone pump
house was coming alive.

～

The pump house was designed in the neo-Renaissance revival style. It
is crisp, balanced, proportionately pleasing from any perspective. The exterior is brick, yellow buff color, the Firestone standard finish. The roof was
originally finished in red tile. Deep overhanging eaves dramatize the shadow
effect, further enlivened by the articulated, carved wood rafter tails.

Built in 1916, the pump house is an elegant reminder of Summit Lake's
leisure days and the only public building still existing from that time on the

eastern shore. Its looks today like a small Italian palazzo was gently deposited on the shore of Summit Lake while no one was paying attention.

However, its exterior grace and refinement contradict its historic purpose. The interior tells a different story. For sixty years, twenty-four hours a day, it sucked water from Summit Lake. The water was piped underground to the Firestone factory buildings for various non-potable purposes. Still on the pump house site are the massive valves, joints, dials, connectors, nipples, and pressure relief gauges. Above the dark, gaping maw of the water intake basin—the screen keeping fish, turtles, plants, and other incidentals from entering the system—sags with branches and dry leaves. Above the works is the apartment of the pump house manager. After the building was decommissioned in 1978, he and his wife continued to live in the building. After he died, his widow lived there until she died in 1997.

The city ended up with the property. It languished for about a decade. In 2010, Let's Grow Akron took occupancy of the fenced-in grounds around the facility for their demonstration gardens, greenhouse, and chicken coops. Akron artist Mark Soppeland curated a group of students in creating "The Unexpected Aquarium" for the pump house. Bright Disneyesque undersea scenes replaced the plain plywood window protectors. An undulating band of color drew the eye upward to the second floor of the building that had lost its purpose but not its grace.

Into this tilled soil, the Seattle-based artist Hunter Franks saw an opportunity. The founder of the League of Creative Interventionists, he had successfully executed his first Knight Foundation grant in Akron and saw the tremendous potential in the Summit Lake neighborhood. He was not alone in this recognition. Reimaging the Civic Commons was focused on elevating a 2.5-mile section of the canal towpath trail from downtown Akron to the Summit Lake Community Center—the pump house was just south of the community center. There would be ripple effects. There would be attention, publicity, money. Hunter pitched another grant submission with the Knight Foundation, entitled "The Summit Lake Arts & Culture Project."

Hunter Franks and the League had created community-enhancing projects all over the country. They had already proven their capacity in Akron. Their first grant, awarded in 2015 entitled *500 Plates*, was just that:

a sit-down dinner for five hundred self-invited folks on the Innerbelt. Focusing on drawing people from all the neighborhoods of Akron, the meal was intended to connect and promote conversation about the future of the soon to be decommissioned highway they gathered upon.

The League was awarded the second grant of $125,000 for their as-yet-undesignated opportunity. The size of the grant for what was still a vague idea is a testament to the League's reputation and to the focus of the grant: Summit Lake. The idea was rehabilitating an existing property into a community center for arts & culture. Meanwhile, in an obvious irony, the only public building on the entire circumference of the Summit Lake shore happened to be the lively Summit Lake Community Center.

In reaching directly into a long-neglected neighborhood, the League nudged its way into a location that needed attention. Its success in getting money through the arts establishment illuminates the question of imported vs. local artists. What is the story and who gets to tell it?

On a scouting trip from Seattle, the League's home base, Hunter Franks and his partner Anne Coivu identified the locale—the pump house. The project became "The Pump House Center for Arts & Culture." Now they needed an on-the-ground presence, someone a lot closer than Seattle. They needed a local. The Knight Grant budget included the hiring of a local project manager.

The League asked Leo to be the project manager for the pump house project. They also hired a local architectural firm to produce plans for the renovation of the first and second floors of the pump house. Through the winter and spring, they consulted with Leo on the programming planned for the summer.

Leo was accustomed to operating with slim resources. It took some time for her to realize that she was indeed in a new league. Hunter Franks encouraged her to "think big" about the programming, and to buy the materials to enlarge the ideas. Build Corps was created as an employment program for teens for the summer. Power tools, T-shirts, stickers, publicity, and salaries were prepared. The kids were identified and hired.

The summer season for the pump house started with a party and demonstration by Build Corps. In coordination with "Reimagining the Civic Commons," it was a great success, a mingling of lots of Akron subcultures. Locals and outsiders wandered on the grounds of the pump house, admiring the views of the lake, and getting tours of the Let's Grow Akron agriculture. They peeked inside the building at the great network of out-sized plumbing. Lots of people came by bicycle on the adjacent towpath—people who otherwise might turn back home at this towpath section, one that included passing between the lake and the housing projects.

The day had vitality, buzz, pep, promise.

Two weeks later all the power tools were stolen from the pump house. A snitch confirmed Leo's suspicions that it was an inside job, a trust viola-tion. She felt betrayed by the kids she thought were friends. She asked for guidance from Duane. First they approached the families directly. No results. Though snitching is a major violation of street law, Duane called the police. This is community, too—a kind of hard grinding out of a clash of cultures, new money in an old place, good intentions and street hustle, different goals, different laws trying to operate in the same landscape.

The neighborhood paid attention. After a tense aftermath of court appearances and community service, the neighborhood saw that Leo, as Duane had done before her, was going to stay with it, keep walking through the tough stuff together. The tools were never retrieved or replaced. But Build Corps made benches, signs, tables, and chairs by hand—and heavy so nothing would move from where it was planted. It worked.

Over the course of the summer, there was an increasing tension between the artists in Seattle and project manager Leo in Akron. Misunderstandings and lack of clarity in the goals of the project began to wear on the team. As part of the grant, the League hosted its out-of-town members for a weekend to show off the Pump House Center for Arts & Culture. They stayed in a downtown hotel. There were meetings with locals about the future of the pump house. Between the meals and field trips, the out-of-town disciples of creative interventions brainstormed ideas for an action.

Together with the local Build Corps teens, the visitors made a tempo-rary "front porch" on an empty lot next to the Pump House. Though no one spoke it, the day felt forced and uncomfortable. The discomfort was reflected in the result—brightly painted tires filled with instant flowers surrounded a plywood platform, a rickety railing, and a rough uninviting bench. It looked and felt alien, too quick and too hip. It said more about the League than anything the neighborhood would find interesting. Residents of Summit Lake used their own front porches. The group of local teens and out of town creatives gathered around the porch for the pictures, and everyone went home.

Before Hunter and Anne landed back on the West Coast, the porch was all but destroyed. When you invite community participation, you will get some rowdy guests. In this instance of neighborhood vandalism, nothing was done to find the perpetrators. It could have been any number of people reacting to the "intervention" by the League of Creative Interventionists.

Frustrated and ready to quit the job, Leo asked her local collaborators to help her through a conference call with Hunter and Anne. She hoped the witnesses would help get her points across, problems she had tried to talk through with Seattle for weeks. She was prepared and willing to lead the final planned project, a photography course for local teens.

She was not willing to manage the added-on idea for the $40,000 balance of the grant money. Hunter and Anne wanted to stage a community meal to coincide with Reimagining the Civic Common's unveiling of the new landscape features at Summit Lake. Leo thought the money, a huge amount for a community like Summit Lake, should go towards renovation of the Pump House—or be turned back to the Knight Foundation. She based her feeling on material from the artists' stated mission: "to transform and activate the building into an active art, event, and performance space."

While the group around the table waited for Seattle to call, Eric Nelson, the director of the SWAG Program, led a prayer for Leo and for the greater good, whatever God had in mind.[14] Leo, always ready to partner with God, was disappointed in six directions with her human partners.

Everyone in the group she summoned that day had experience in the ways of grant money, that no one on the Akron end of the coming phone call had any influence in how the remaining cash would be spent. They were there to support Leo—and her initial journey into an understanding of how things worked. Without much need to say it, her advisors knew that change is measured over a longer time than anyone would like. Motives are different but intentions can unite. They demonstrated to her that respect and listening is a better servant than alienation. The conversation, if nothing else, let Hunter and Anne know that Leo had friends ready to come to her defense.

By the end of the call, there was agreement that Leo would lead the photo project, but they would find someone else to manage the two-hundred plate "last supper," the sopping up of the grant gravy.

A month later, Leo and the photography students prepared for the exhibition of their work. The photo show opening was two days before the two-hundred plate dinner. Local photographer Shane Wynn's large format pictures of Summit Lake residents lined the towpath from the community center to the pump house. It was a beautiful evening on Summit Lake. On the grounds of the pump house, there was live music, lemonade, and copies of the hardbound book of the students' work. Hunter and Leo made brief remarks. There were tons of kids, teens, and Summit Lake locals. Almost everyone walked to get there. The teens forgot they had to be cool. They ran around signing their names on the pages with their work.

Even the power tool thieves were there, working the lemonade dispenser, part of the community. Whatever tension it took to get to that point, it was not remotely in evidence. It was a light and seemingly effortless evening. It cost a lot to get there, but something had shifted. It was community. It was real—it was art.

By this time, Hunter and Anne had started to work on the third Knight Foundation grant, $214,000 to create a pop-up forest on the decommissioned and partially demolished Innerbelt. Their involvement with the pump house was over.

As Duane and Lisa walked along Summit Lake on the towpath towards home after the event, they were happy. This event in particular made them realize that good things were happening, things they had no role in. Their only involvement was showing up to celebrate.

This was not the same place they had moved to twenty years before with the big ideas. They stopped to take in the view of the new shoreline created through the Civic Commons project. It was a sandy beach, bordered by huge Berea sandstone boulders and dotted with benches in the margin between the grass and the lake. They watched people doing just what they were doing, enjoying a beautiful night in a beautiful place within a walk's distance from home.

The river is shaped like a child's drawing of a smile.

How do things change, through what source does transformation emerge? Maybe it's a shift of light, drawing attention to something not seen before. Maybe it's the bravery of one voice becoming a chorus that does it. Maybe it is someone, not knowing any better, who wanders in and asks why that big guy forgot to put his clothes on that day. Maybe it's just a matter of time that brings the conditions for change.

Something that was unremarkable gets noticed. Called out, the invisible thing is finally seen and is no longer acceptable.

With the Cuyahoga River, the cost of doing business meant the river got dirty. The current kept flowing, if sluggishly, so the lake got dirty. When the river caught fire on June 22, 1969, it was unremarkable. The fire was only newsworthy because the flames damaged two bridges. Even at that, the story warranted a few unattributed paragraphs in the back section of the *Cleveland Plain Dealer*. Burning debris on the surface was common.

Like my older brothers and sisters, I learned to swim in Lake Erie. There were days when the beach was one massive sheet of dead fish, days of intense green seaweed, and days where the shoreline was scored with thick black goo from one of those long freighters on the horizon traveling the St. Lawrence Seaway. We just moved it aside to clear a path to the open water past the effluent. There plenty of other days in the mix. When the lake was "fun rough" we'd bounce and roll around the edges, bathing suits sagging, full of small stones. Other days, the water was flat blue calm, glass clear, giving over to a whole new set of underwater games. That was the lake we knew and loved.

We lost our connection to the lake in 1963. After the sudden death of our father, it seemed best to sell the little summer cottage in Madison, Ohio. Our personal loss came five years before the slogan "Lake Erie is dead" gained popularity.

Then the river caught fire.

With that fire, the time had come that such things could no longer be considered the cost of doing business. The environmental movement took shape around the burning river. Perhaps the contradiction of fire feeding on water grated against a shared primal spirit, something so against the natural flow it could no longer be ignored. Collectively, we had to take action.

I was fifteen on the first Earth Day March in Cleveland, the spring after the river caught fire. It's possible I would not remember the march were it not for my cousin's friend. She stole a gas station attendant's belt clip change dispenser. It was full of coins, and she wore it like a trophy the rest of the march. Lacking the courage to stand up to that kind of cool, I felt bad. I didn't have any means to describe the taint of complicity, sadness, and shame. The day just took a dark turn. I felt it through my hands holding up the poster board protest sign. It was another incomprehensible moment heaped onto the unrecognized urgency of getting away from the place I was born. Leaving seemed the only way for me to change what was unseen and invisible in my personal story, a fenced-off forbidden void of the erased father.

~

Forty-five years later, I was back in the Cuyahoga River valley. At the invitation of Cleveland artist Kathy Skerritt, I stood in a small circle of people beside a calm green lake, the headwaters of the Cuyahoga River. We listened as Sharon Day described the purpose of the next four days.

"We carry the river from the headwaters, where it is pure and clean to where the river flows into Lake Erie, to remind her of what she was at the beginning."

It was that that simple and that profound.

Sharon is a water walker and Ojibwe elder. She led us with a boundless trust. In the quiet steady flow, she exposed a space of awe and gratitude that billowed in the motion itself. We were in the flow of conscious immediacy through the continuous act of carrying the river in a copper vessel. We sang to, prayed for, and gave thanks to the water over the eighty-mile walking meditation.

The silences within the day's walking got longer. The laughter, in the evenings over food together, grew deeper. By the third day, the world around us became part of the experience. Everything had a voice. Even the mailboxes lined along a suburban street sang as we passed.

On the afternoon of the fourth day, we passed through the last part of the river's course before she meets the lake. This is the industrial valley of Cleveland. The river is constricted in a deep channel and encased in the harsh beauty of steel. We moved through that bright angularity of submission still in a song, a dissonant cadence with its own surprising beauty. Everything belonged.

We were joined by others as we got closer to the lake. It started raining. We crossed through territory indifferent to walkers, over rail lines, through the tunneled freeway underpass, at last on Whiskey Island, flowing parallel now with the still invisible great lake just to our left. Picking up speed as the rain grew heavier, we moved steadily, silently, towards the strategic port of entry, the mouth of the Cuyahoga River.

At the brink of land giving over to water, a group of native musicians stood waiting in the rain. We had arrived at the transition point of the river. Immediately before us, the river flowed left, north, squarely through steel-sheeted ribs. We turned sharply with it, drawn faster by the intensity of the river, the rain, the wind, and the drumming. The perspective snapped open wide to the lake and sky. The pier stretched thin in the tension between land, river, and the Coast Guard station at its end. Our passage narrowing even as we moved into the expansion of water and sky.

The journey was over. At the terminal point, the transformation seemed instant to me. Suddenly we were a powerless raggedy group in a raggedy circle, a tiny dot. The June-chilled wind off the lake snatched at everything: voices, drums, clothes, and smudge pot smoke, pulling, scrubbing our faces. We were standing at the lowest point of land in Northeast Ohio, where the Cuyahoga River moves into Lake Erie, all vulnerable and naked beneath a nuanced gray of enormous expanse.

Above and behind us, the ineffective jabs of jackknife bridges and brick stacks reached up under the equally ineffective stands of downtown towers. Nothing human beings had shoved in the soil could compare to the confluence of these bodies of water and that sky. The folly of believing that we controlled nature was inescapable.

Sharon gave Kathy the honor of tipping the copper vessel of the river into the river, the reminder of who she was when she started.

It is as simple as it is profound.

Furious reversals of wind snuffed the candles held behind cupped hands and hunched backs. The Coast Guard Station offered no protection. Standing near the compact mass of the building, what had always seemed gossamer from a distance was ordinary and modest. At last, the Coast Guard station had found me. As a child, I always looked forward to a fleeting glance as we sped along the Lakeshore Freeway on the trips to the west side of Cleveland to see relatives. They were only glimpses, but enough to feel the obsolete grandeur in the lines of it, the whiteness of it, facing the lake with all its ghostly, remote, inaccessible charm.

There was no sound save our feeble voices and the wind that scattered the sound in a weak bandwidth of fractured poetry. Had the lake erupted in one of her famous sudden squalls, we would have all been swept away— the river walkers, the Native American musicians, the urban families fishing that day, the ground-in bait. Every other loose thing had already been taken.

But we were deeply rooted in the world of our creation. We had gained something together in these days with Sharon and the river, a something mutually felt. It was right there with us, in that thin space, that slice between water, land and sky. Right there, in nature's eyeblink, the river shook the blanket of our attempts to colonize her wildness.

How foolish it suddenly was, the idea that we killed Lake Erie.

Before then I thought I believed in resurrection. But in the moments together on the pier I knew it as real, without any attachment to human efforts. Resurrection's indifference is its grace. That simple and that profound.

Camille gasped. From her point on the circle, she faced the full brunt of the wind. Her hair streamed out behind the fullness of expression. Her face glowed with awe in the surprised delight of a fish jumping in the air above Lake Erie.

Notes

1. Bible, King James Version, Exodus, 3:5.
2. Wilson, Bill, "In Memory of Sister Ignatia," AA Grapevine, New York, NY, August 1966.
3. Ian Lewis, Inner Circle, "Bad Boys," One Way, 1987.
4. The first gathering in an airport hotel of 189 people grew to over 5,000 by the convention in 2017, held in the Renaissance Center in Detroit, Michigan.
5. Akron Commission on Civil Disorders assessment, April 16, 1969.
6. Robenalt, James, *Ballots and Bullets, Black Power Politics and Urban Guerrilla Warfare in 1968 Cleveland* (Lawrence Hill Books, 2018), 242.
7. "Text of Housing Ruling in Akron School Suit," *Akron Beacon Journal*, Wednesday, April 9, 1980.
8. "Drug-fighting group inspired AMHA grant but won't benefit," *Akron Beacon Journal*, September 29, 1990.
9. Proposition 8 was a California Ballot Proposition and state constitutional amendment passed in November 2008. The measure countermanded the intention of the State Supreme Court's ruling legalizing same-sex marriage. After lengthy subsequent suits, Prop 8 was effectively declared unconstitutional by the Federal Ninth Circuit Court on June 28, 2013,

allowing Governor Jerry Brown to order the resumption of same-sex marriages in the State of California.

10.   The Christian Community Development Association, (CCDA) was founded by John Perkins and Wayne Gordon. Duane was present at the first gathering of the organization in Chicago in 1989.

11.   https://www.arts.gov/about

12.   The statue controversy extended beyond its original outrage around the Confederate figures. The sculptor of the Harvey statue, James Earl Fraser, had created a striking bronze composition of Theodore Roosevelt astride a horse flanked by two walking companions. It towers on the stairs leading to the entry doors of the Natural History Museum in New York. Theodore is ecstatic, towering above the massive horse beneath him and the two companions, a Black man and a Native American.

13.   After the Charlottesville, North Carolina City Council voted to remove the statue of Robert E. Lee and rename the eponymous park "Emancipation Park" opponents of the removal started demonstrating. The tension escalated when counter-demonstrations supporting the removal began. A man opposing the removal drove his car straight into those supporting the removal, killing Heather Heyer and injuring twenty-eight people.

14.   I was present along with Veronica Sims, Council at Large of the Akron City Council, Eric Nelson, head of the SWAG program, Grace Hudson, a long standing neighborhood activist, and Lisa Nunn, Director of Let's Grow Akron.

Photo: Shane Wynn

Mary O'Connor is an architect who specialized in public assembly spaces in her twenty-five-year practice in New York City. Prior to becoming an architect, she was an aquatic comedian and hostess at Manhattan Plaza Health Club. Her career came to an abrupt conclusion after a near drowning incident during an act that featured diving off the board in a full evening gown. She moves through the world via seven bicycles in four cities.

Printed in the United States
by Baker & Taylor Publisher Services